**WALL
STREET
JOURNAL
BOOKS**

CONTENTS

Contents

For my dad, who set me on the right career path and gobbled up
every word I ever wrote until Alzheimer's robbed him
of the ability to do so . . .

PROMOTING YOURSELF

52 Lessons for Getting to the Top...
and Staying There

HAL LANCASTER

A WALL STREET JOURNAL BOOK

PUBLISHED BY SIMON & SCHUSTER

New York   London   Toronto   Sydney   Singapore

WALL
STREET
JOURNAL
BOOKS

A WALL STREET JOURNAL BOOK
Published by Simon & Schuster, Inc.
Rockefeller Center
1230 Avenue of the Americas
New York, NY 10020

For information about special discounts for bulk purchases,
please contact Simon & Schuster Special Sales:
1-800-456-6798 or business@simonandschuster.com

Book design by Susan Hood

Manufactured in the United States of America

10 9 8 7 6 5 4 3 2 1

Library of Congress Cataloging-in-Publication Data

Lancaster, Hal.
Promoting yourself : 52 lessons for getting to the top—and staying there /
Hal Lancaster.
p. cm.—(Wall Street journal book)
Includes index.
1. Career development. 2. Promotions. I. Title. II. Series.
HF5381 .L2883 2002
650.14—dc21   2001049776
ISBN 0-7432-1363-7

PREFACE

Welcome to the career guide for people who hate career guides. You know the books I'm talking about: *How to Get a Raise in 30 Minutes; How to Become a CEO in 30 Days or Less; Follow Your Passion to Achieve Career Bliss.* The shelves at your local bookstore are groaning with career/leadership/management tomes penned by the latest hot headhunter, executive career adviser, football coach, or motivational flimflammer. You can get leadership lessons from *Star Trek,* a success primer from Winnie-the-Pooh, and management tips from Moses— really! I'm waiting for *The 7 Habits of Highly Effective Dictators* by Fidel Castro or *Management by Bullying* by Bobby Knight.

Have these career gurus ever lived on this planet? If they did, they'd know their simplistic formulas for career success don't work for everyone. All of you who have toiled in the messy, chaotic vineyards of work know the task of building a career is replete with ups and downs, hurdles and roadblocks, luck and misfortune. Along the way, you pit your skills and competitive fire against a horde of ambitious bosses, peers, and subordinates, all seeking to grab the brass ring of career success. Some will play fair, others won't, and justice won't always prevail. The workplace isn't a pure meritocracy, as much as we'd like it to be (that goes for your workplace, too, you high-tech dreamers).

But that doesn't mean you can't prosper and be happy while doing it. You just need to know the possibilities available to you and then make the best possible choices. That's what this book is all about. What I am offering is a commonsense road map to the issues that really matter in building a successful management career: How can you find the right job? How can you make your job better? When should you dump your current job? How can you survive your boss's many quirks and foibles? How do you maneuver through the political quicksand that makes corporate life so treacherous? What alternate paths to glory exist, and what do you need to know to follow them? How can you make sense of all the mergers, technological advances, and cultural mutations that have muddied the career waters? How can you be an effective leader through all these shifting circumstances?

I know a little something about this, having been both a participant and an observer on the front lines of business for thirty years as a reporter and editor for *The Wall Street Journal*. And for five years I wrote the *Journal*'s weekly "Managing Your Career" column. I'm currently writing a similar column for the *Journal*'s CareerJournal website.

So what will you find lurking in these pages? It won't be convenient buzzwords about empowerment and owning your job, which bear little resemblance to corporate reality. There won't be any paradigm shifting on my watch (if my paradigm shifts one more time, I'll need a chiropractor). I won't kill any trees expounding on the wonders of the two-paragraph cover letter. Entire books are already devoted to that riveting subject. We won't be exploring the soul in the workplace, and I won't promise you health, wealth, and the mate of your dreams in thirty minutes or less.

This book is for those folks who are as bewildered as I am by the training gurus who collect big bucks for convincing people that they can build a smooth corporate team and advance their careers by walking on a wire or tramping through the woods. It's for people who question the quick-fix psychobabble served up by the empowered, self-actualized, spirituality-seeking nexus that now dominates the overstuffed career advice field.

This is a book not for dummies or complete idiots, but for accomplished managers and highly skilled professionals seeking fulfilling careers. It recognizes that as much as things have changed—and they have—many essential truths about careers remain the same. It recognizes that there are no magic rules of conduct that will transform you into Jack Welch overnight.

But make no mistake about it: This is a book about people seeking a path to career success. And that means wildly different things to different people. For some, it's more important to be an integral part of their children's lives and to support their spouse's careers. They're willing to sacrifice their own advancement to be there when their family needs them. These are certainly people to be admired.

Others want to steam ahead at full speed, even if it means sacrificing parts of their lives. They won't be at all the soccer games and school plays. They'll often combine vacation and business. They will undoubtedly cross swords with their spouses now and again over whose career takes precedence.

Keep that in mind as you read this book, and ignore the incessant bleating of the work-family mafia, who insist that you must always place family and children above all else. All that matters is what works for you and your family. Sometimes—not always, or even most of the time—the needs of your career must take precedence over the needs of your family. I once wrote that there are times you must say to your kids, "No, I can't play with you, I have to work now." Such heresy earned me several scathing letters, which, in essence, damned me as the Antichrist and insisted that I promptly surrender my children to the nearest authorities.

But for many of us, careers are important and fulfilling. And if your career is a major priority, it doesn't mean you're a bad person. Nobody can do it all, not man, or woman, or beast. If you plan it well, you can be there for most of it. If you've married and parented well, and frequently demonstrated your enduring love to your family, they will understand the rest. Finally, this book is constructed on the notion that you learn best not by listening to the ramblings of so-called experts, but by studying the experiences of others like you who have been through the business wars.

Most of what you will read here comes from the real-life experiences of managers and professionals I have interviewed over the years. Their stories reflect the often baffling contradictions of the business world and offer no pat formulas for career success.

One caveat: It is highly likely that many of the sources cited herein have moved on to other positions since we crossed paths. Since up-to-the-minute descriptions were impossible, given the harsh realities of deadlines in the book-publishing world, I decided to leave them where I originally found them.

Hopefully, in the ensuing chapters, we can show you some of the roads to success others have taken and some of the principles they followed. Many of them, I hope, will resonate with you and offer templates for your own career. Some of them won't. So be it. You choose what might work for you.

INTRODUCTION

So what's the story here? Are we in the midst of career utopia, a world of never-ending opportunity sparked by the wonders of the Internet and high technology? Or is this just another illusion, already yielding to the usual boom-and-bust economic cycle?

After a decade that started in recession and the career-altering era of reengineering and ended in Internet euphoria and stock option jackpots, what can we count on in our careers at the dawn of the new millennium? For what kind of world must we prepare?

Even at the height of dotcomania, the American workplace embraced wildly conflicting and confusing trends. While skilled techies job-hopped with glee as talent-starved companies dished out obscene signing bonuses, stock options, and pay hikes to lure people away from rivals, boatloads of older managers were quietly being ushered out the back door despite healthy corporate profits.

Then came "the Great Dotcom Crash of Double Aught," when seemingly overnight the investment community awoke from mass Internet hysteria and remembered the rules of business economics. Apparently we all weren't going to hook up to an Internet whirlwind, cash in our stock options, and retire gazillionaires at twenty-five. In the cold light of day, in fact, the dotcom paradise envisioned by so many turned out to be riddled with just as much uncertainty, politics, and bureaucracy as the mainstream corporations they had abandoned. Quietly, many of those who rashly ran away and joined the Internet circus, fearful of missing out on the "next big thing," started looking for a safe route home.

How you fared in this confluence of swirling career winds depended on your age, industry, skills, and luck. For Lana Sanderson, born of the last generation and its giant corporations, the 1990s were a time of turmoil, unemployment, attempted career changes, and a struggle to at least get back what she had lost. For Jennifer Geissel, who started her career in an Internet wonderland, it was a decade of choices and abundant opportunity, amid a growing realization that the fairy tale couldn't continue forever.

Their divergent stories illustrate many of the forces that have shaped the current career picture in corporate America and, more important, where we're headed from here.

———

I met Lana Sanderson at an outplacement industry conference in 1994. She was a Ciba-Geigy sales manager with a proven track record who watched helplessly as her Spokane, Washington, office was consolidated in a major restructuring. She was suddenly forty-four years old, a divorced mother of two teenagers, unemployed, and totally confused. Why was this happening in America? Didn't companies owe longtime employees more loyalty than this?

She paid her own way to the conference to put these questions to the so-called experts. I was struck by this quest and wrote one of my first columns about her.

Over the next five years, Ms. Sanderson struggled to find a new place in the career firmament. Disillusioned with the corporate world (like so many others), she decided to satisfy a long-held urge to write. A magazine for entrepreneurs hired her to write a monthly column on working at home, but it "fed my ego better than it fed my family," she says.

In 1995, she landed what seemed to be a dream job as director of training and curriculum development for Krypton International, a start-up firm that franchised a training program for small businesses. Here she was, on the cutting edge of the entrepreneurial movement, developing business courses that enabled her to use the teaching skills she considered her greatest strength as a manager. Plus, company founder Berry Fowler, a serial entrepreneur who had previously launched the successful Sylvan Learning Centers, retained her to ghostwrite his autobiography. She only got a "modest" paycheck, but she got an equity stake and percentages of book and franchise sales.

By God, the gurus were right. If you pursued your passion, success would inevitably follow. Here she was, in a position that allowed her to do her two favorite things—teaching and writing—with a pot of gold at the end of the rainbow to boot. "If it had taken off," she says, "I'd be sitting pretty."

It didn't. The company foundered, and in 1997, Ms. Sanderson found herself back at square one. She took some time off to tend to sick parents (her father died that year). "I felt lucky that I wasn't working," she says. "I felt guilty when I wasn't with my kids and guilty when I wasn't with my parents, but I would have felt much more guilty if I didn't have the time to spend with my parents."

Eventually, there were bills to be paid, and what did she really have to offer an employer? Looking at her career pragmatically, she saw a pharmaceutical sales professional with a solid track record. Besides, she found she missed the camaraderie of the corporate team and the self-esteem boost she got from corporate life. Saying she was a free-lance writer "didn't feel like work," she says. It lacked the heft of saying you were a manager with a prestigious pharmaceutical company.

Fortuitously, the rebounding pharmaceutical industry was in a hiring mood again. Still stinging from her past experience, she cast about for the most solid, reliable company she could find and landed a sales rep job with good old reliable Merck in September 1997.

Getting back to the managerial level has been slower. Merck prefers a long developmental process and has a wealth of managerial candidates. Ciba-Geigy used assessment centers to pluck out managerial candidates, a process that helped her become a manager in just eighteen months.

It seems now to be just a matter of time, however. Her name has been put on the "promotable audit," a prerequisite for managerial jobs, and she has started interviewing for sales manager jobs in various Merck divisions.

Her lost half decade cost her a great deal financially. "I missed out on that phenomenal period of stock market growth that made a lot of people rich," she says.

Now, for the first time, she will receive stock options, standard for Merck managers. "I'm looking forward to having golden handcuffs," she says.

Now her children are gone. Her son, Dan, is a thoroughly modern college dropout—that is, he dropped out to sign a lucrative contract as a programmer with a huge entertainment company, complete with signing bonus and options. It's now time for her to focus on her career, and she's approaching it with a different attitude: less deferential to authority, more appreciative of stability, less prone to anxiety attacks.

"You get out of school, you get a job, you know you can't have gaps in your employment or you'll be unemployable," she says. "There's a feeling you can't stop, and I probably wouldn't have if I hadn't been kicked off the treadmill. I know myself so much better now."

If Ms. Sanderson's experience represents the older generation's plight in today's workplace, Jennifer Geissel's demonstrates how wild and strange the world has become for the younger generation.

Ms. Geissel worked her way through college as a secretary for Donaldson, Lufkin & Jenrette, the big investment banker. When she graduated in 1992, DLJ put her into a two-year training program, promising to hire her as an investment banking associate if she did well. She did and they did. This admittedly "back-door" entry in this elite business earned her some resentment from the "Wharton number jocks" she was working beside.

"The first six months, I worked harder than anybody," she recalls. "I slept there the first weekend."

By the time she was twenty-five, she was earning $100,000 a year. Still, her unorthodox background bugged her. "I worked my tail off, but I knew I wasn't great," she says.

To polish her skills and gain confidence, she decided to go to business school, immersing herself in a full-time program at Dartmouth's Amos Tuck School of Business. "My family thought I was nuts," she says. "'Why give up $100,000 a year? Go to school at night.'"

But in the world she was entering, credentials meant a lot, particularly an Ivy League MBA. It got you in the door for job interviews at elite companies. And you went into those interviews knowing an aura of accomplishment surrounded you even before the first question was asked.

"This was a whole new world, and I had to ride that wave," she says. "I needed that validation. I wasn't coming from an Ivy League undergraduate school, but I was in an Ivy League world."

Unlike others who proceeded from that realization directly to start-up fever, Ms. Geissel cast about for a safer route. "I've always taken the safe route," she says. "It's hard for me to take that kind of risk."

Upon graduating from Tuck, she hooked on with a strategy consulting firm for a year and got her Internet indoctrination. She then moved to Treacy & Co., a small start-up founded by Michael Treacy, an MIT Sloan business professor and the coauthor of *The Discipline of Market Leaders.* That company was eventually merged into Gen3 Partners.

This wasn't an ordinary consulting firm. They didn't just advise, they constructed. Ms. Geissel's assignment, for example, was to launch Internet divisions for old-line companies. "Here, I can take all these operating roles and still get the support system of a well-funded organization with strong thinkers behind me," she explains. But she also got equity, not only in Gen3, but in the Internet businesses she created.

At last, it seemed she had arrived; when she spoke, people listened. "Because I look young, I used to be the last person they looked to for answers at meetings," she says. "Now I've got more Internet experience than others at my company."

But as she gathered with fellow Tuck graduates for a seminar in 1999, she was in the process of career decompression. After a chaotic three years of building companies and wealth, she was slowing down to consider her future. "I was exhausted," she says. Around her, the organization was changing, too, having nearly tripled its workforce in the previous five months. A layer of vice presidents was created just above her.

She decided to take a month off and consider her options. "Half the people in this room have equity stakes in something," she says. She tells of colleagues who started their own virtual consulting firm in Vermont. "Until recently, you had to work for McKinsey to sell a case," she says.

The pressure to do something big is building before this ship—no, make that this monstrous ocean liner—departs. Ms. Geissel wonders what the value of all those equity stakes will be in five years. Already, some friends' companies have failed. "Business-to-consumer Internet companies are dead now, and business-to-business is next," she says.

Since then, the carnage has escalated and the younger generation has joined its elder in a state of confusion. "What keeps me up nights is, what's next?"

That's keeping everybody up. It's why you're reading this book. There are answers to the questions posed by Ms. Sanderson and Ms. Geissel, but they're not perfect answers, and one size definitely doesn't fit all. Some of the rules of the career game have changed, but others remain steadfastly the same. In the ensuing chapters, we'll apprise you of the former and remind you of the latter. We'll show you many of the options available to you at various stages of your career and raise the questions you need to ask yourself about each. The rest is up to you.

Careers never develop predictably; use every surprising twist and turn to re-evaluate where you want to go and why.

PART ONE

———

SELLING YOURSELF

WHITHER GOEST RÉSUMÉS?

When I first started writing about careers, I vowed that I wouldn't waste much time pondering the intricacies of résumés. After all, there was already a surplus of weighty tomes on the subject. These books professed to reveal the secrets to penning résumés that would "knock 'em dead," "knock your socks off," be "trashproof," or just be "damn good."

Besides, I grumped one morning at the breakfast table, what's the magic in writing a good résumé? Be clear, truthful, and brief, and sprinkle liberally with evidence of your accomplishments.

It took my wife about two minutes to set me straight. "Writing a résumé is easy for you," she said. "You're a writer. For most of us, it's torture. Look at me. I've got to write about holding eight different jobs with one employer, counting promotions, and I've got to keep it to one page. But if it's all jammed up, they'll just toss it right into the trash can without reading it."

Okay, so maybe there is something to this résumé angst. Unfortunately, much of the blather being dished out on this topic is just plain wrongheaded, in my humble opinion. In one article, for example, a well-known résumé guru, who shall be unnamed, advises candidates how to make themselves more appealing on paper "without actually lying," even if they fail to meet the requirements of a position.

The secret, he adds, is to "stylize and summarize." For example, if your objective is to become sales manager, he says, for God's sake, don't say that. Say you're "seeking a challenging and responsible position as a sales manager, where ability, training, and experience can be most effectively and profitably utilized." Here's another one: In summarizing your employment history, don't just say you "hired, trained, supervised, and motivated subordinate staff." Instead, say you "efficiently hired, strategically trained, cost-effectively supervised, and objectively motivated subordinate staff."

Oh, please. Would you hire the pretentious windbag who wrote that? Can you really get a job by inserting puffy adjectives in front of all your nouns? Besides, do most employers think you're after an unchallenging and irresponsible position where your ability, training, and experience can be ineffectively and unprofitably utilized? And anyone can say he hired efficiently and trained strategically, etc., etc., but can he prove it?

In truth, even the greatest work of the genre isn't likely to get you a job; the best it can do is get you in the door, and even in that task it is frequently supplanted by a good company contact. In the ultimate hiring decision, your interview and references carry far more weight. However, a really bad résumé can indeed cost you a job, by eliminating you from contention before you get a chance to dazzle.

But job hunting may not even be the best reason for maintaining an up-to-date résumé. At its best, a résumé is a flexible marketing tool that will not only aid in your job search, but help you manage your career between searches. Writing one forces you to define your career goals. It's a repository for samples of your best work, available upon request to prospective employers and for your own use in gauging current work progress and preparing for performance reviews and promotions.

This obviously can be a massive document, and you certainly don't want to pass on the *War and Peace* of résumés to time-challenged hiring managers. Most of all, hiring managers want simplicity and brevity. Wouldn't you, if you had a stack of those documents piled to the ceiling? "If it's over two pages, I'm not going to read it," says Alston Gardner, CEO of Atlanta's Target Marketing Systems. "I don't have that big an attention span."

They want to be able to trace your job and education history eas-ily, they want some proof that you can do the job you're seeking, and they don't want to see unexplained gaps in your history or any ques-tions that set off their red-flag radar. That's it.

So what can you do, within those parameters, to cut yourself out of the herd? I won't promise you anything that will "knock their socks off"; frankly, I'm not so sure that's a good thing, if you catch my drift. But the key here is to replace vagaries with specifics. Most résumés fall short by focusing on a dry recitation of jobs held and meaningless proclamations of competency. Hiring managers want to see facts and figures that will make them feel comfortable in handing you the key to the executive washroom. Most résumés I've seen fail to provide sufficient proof of accomplishments. It's fine to state you have an excellent record in doing such and such, but everyone else is stating that, too. How is a hiring manager to know who's the real deal and who's blowing smoke?

So let's pretend you're the hiring manager. Which would you rather see:

A. Efficiently hired, strategically trained, cost-effectively supervised, and objectively motivated subordinate staff.

B. In my two years as manager of the widget department, I initiated a cost-control program and an intense sales training effort. As a result, the department's sales increased 25 percent, while costs declined 10 percent.

If you answered A, close this book immediately and go find that résumé writer.

If you're still reading, congratulations. You've passed the windbag test.

Here are some other ideas for sprucing up your résumé: What did you do that earned you a promotion, raise, or bonus? What division did you retool? If you have accomplishments that relate directly to your prospective employer's business, all the better. If you've got a great story that illustrates your management style and how it bene-fited the company in some way, tell it (try to keep it brief, however). Anecdotes are even more powerful than numbers; they hit people in the gut in a way that numbers never can. Do you have a turnaround story, some unit that was rescued from the Dumpster under your brilliant stewardship? Everybody loves a turnaround story.

But numbers aren't bad, either. What projects did you complete that added x percent to the bottom line or saved x percent in costs, and what specifically did you contribute to that success? What successful new products or services did you launch, and how much did they add to the company's revenues and profits?

My other bit of advice about résumés is detailed in the next chapter: Something you didn't anticipate—something you might even consider irrelevant to your current job search—might be just the ticket to a new career. So don't dismiss any past experience without examining its possible ramifications to some new employer. These potential job winners can be almost anything: organizing a fundraising campaign for your church or club; seminars you attended and classes you took; leadership roles in school or in professional organizations; a report you wrote or a particular project you took on for another employer. "What works," said Tim Jones, vice president of human resources for Forte Software, Oakland, California, "is what tells your story relative to the needs of the organization."

To listen to some gurus who extol the virtues of networking or narrative letters over résumés, you'd think the genre was dead. Mr. Jones illustrates the fallacy in such thinking. He notes that it isn't unusual to be hired without a résumé in the Bay Area, especially in hot technical areas. Forte, for example, offers bonuses to employee recruiters. "It's all word of mouth," he says. "You know where they've been, their areas of expertise, the product they've developed—and the résumé is superfluous." Having said that, he concedes that résumés serve as "the prelude to a person's candidacy" in an estimated 90 percent of hirings at Forte. Likewise, while unsolicited résumés almost never lead to job offers at Target Marketing, which relies on search firms and personal references, Mr. Gardner says candidates are expected to have them.

Both employers like to see facts on achievements—such as sales figures or quotas that have been attained—in the résumé, as long as they're concise. Beyond that, common sense rules. You need to constantly edit and customize your résumé, Mr. Gardner says. You'll also need a separate résumé larded with so-called key words—buzzwords programmed into computer screening programs to identify likely job candidates and eliminate those lacking the needed qualifications.

So let's review. By maintaining a continually updated résumé, complete with a log of past work and life experiences and a portfolio of samples of your best work, you will have a tool that helps you define your career goals and prepare you for performance reviews and other career discussions. And you will be more than ready to draft résumés when the time comes for job hunting.

Since employers prize brevity, this compendium of your work life must be pared and parsed, customized for each prospective employer by selecting the accomplishments from your past that best fit the profile of skills and knowledge that employer is seeking. And if you've been diligent in maintaining a complete inventory of educational experiences, training, workshops, projects, reports, and extracurricular activities, you will have a wealth of material from which to choose.

If you're up on your technology, by now you're asking yourself, What about electronic résumés and databases and the like? What should I do about them in this age of cyber-recruiting? Well, read on. That discussion is coming up shortly.

Résumé\'re-zə-,mā\ *n. 1: a brief and flexible document recounting one's education and career that is updated continually whether used or not; 2: a turgid and self-serving document that tells someone else something about you that you didn't want them to know. (continued)*

2

Highlighting hidden skills

You can sift through the thousands of volumes penned about career management. You can pay a small fortune for psychological testing and career counseling. You can schmooze and work your contacts until your tongue falls out.

And even then you may not be able to fathom that wondrous, miraculous little something that finally nudges a hiring manager into hiring you. Why? Because sometimes, what finally wins the day is something so well hidden, you aren't even aware of its power.

For Tony Sanger, it was his pilot's license. He sent his résumé to Kenneth Razak, who ran a small consulting engineering business that often created three-dimensional models to aid in providing expert testimony. The pilot's license, Mr. Razak explained, convinced him that Mr. Sanger, who otherwise had scant experience in the field, would be adept at visualizing things in three dimensions.

The truth of the matter is, when you're putting together a résumé, you can't always tell what will seal the deal. Mr. Sanger considered the pilot's license so irrelevant to the job, he left it off his résumé. It surfaced only during the interview.

I recall a major headhunter telling me that one of his clients cut a senior executive out of a herd of similarly trained rivals because he discovered, from the résumé, that he had been a volunteer in a political campaign and that he had been captain of his college baseball team. To him, that translated into leadership skills.

The lesson here is to keep an inventory of all your experiences and skills. One of them may someday land you the career of your dreams.

It's equally important to keep updating that inventory with new experiences—projects you took on, conferences you attended, training and education you received. Because over time, those memories will surely fade. Quick, can you remember every project, seminar, or class you took even ten years ago?

Mr. Razak has been preaching the gospel for decades, since he headed Kansas's industrial extension service. "I learned there were a lot of people in this state who didn't have degrees but had done a lot of learning," he says. So he developed what he called the Lifetime Learning Transcript, on which you can dutifully record all the projects, seminars, workshops, conferences, volunteer work, on-the-job training, and life experiences that constitute your body of knowledge. "A résumé can show people what school you attended," he says, "but it doesn't give the receiver any idea of what you can do."

Others have proposed similar career information–gathering devices, usually called career portfolios. They're adjuncts to résumés that can be useful in chronicling the things you've learned for prospective employers and in preparing you for your job interview.

Of course, with that wealth of information at your disposal, as stated in the last chapter, you must resist dumping it all into your résumé. Instead, do your research—job descriptions in classifieds and on websites, conversations with contacts at the company. Define the qualities and experiences the company is seeking for this position, then comb through your inventory for items that fit the profile. The inventory provides a database that will allow you to customize your résumé for each prospective employer—or at least for the serious ones.

For further proof of the power of hidden assets, we return to Mr. Sanger, who, after his stint with Mr. Razak's firm and, for a while, with the company that bought the engineering consultancy, applied for a design engineer's job with a Wichita construction company. His hopes weren't high, since design engineers were, in his words, "a dime a dozen" and he hadn't completed his engineering degree. But when the interviewer discovered, during their conversation, that Mr. Sanger had experience with scheduling software, something that could solve one of construction's never-ending problems, he hired him immediately.

As the eminent American philosopher Roseanne Roseannadanna put it, "It just goes to show you, it's always something."

Résumé (continued) 3: A brief and flexible document that shows a potential employer exactly what you can do for his or her company.

3

PROMOTING YOURSELF ONLINE

It's the age of computers and software and the Internet, so why the heck are we still killing trees to write résumés?

Well, that's just another aspect of the so-called paperless office that has never come to pass, so you might as well get used to it, at least for another decade or so. But that doesn't mean you shouldn't be using the resources technology has laid at your feet to promote your career.

What can you find there? Ask Scott R. Lucado, an undercover operative in the technological wars. His assignment: to gather intelligence on the products and services of competitors and potential clients. His favorite tool: Internet help-wanted ads.

Companies tell "a great deal about their technology in help-wanted ads," says Mr. Lucado, of Fort Worth, who consults with companies on the use of the Internet for intelligence gathering. "Sometimes I wonder whether organizations realize how much sensitive information seeps out."

He was once asked to do a report on rumors that rivals of his then employer were about to introduce new speech-recognition products. But Mr. Lucado didn't find any hiring activity outside of research laboratories. Further checking from various sources confirmed that no significant new products were on the horizon.

You can also gather intelligence through newsgroups devoted to specific industries or trades, virtual on-line communities formed to discuss, well, almost anything. To search for newsgroups, go to deja.com, or go to websites such as Vault.com, which profess to be the business world's cyber–water cooler, where people gather to gossip and trade intelligence about their companies. Here you can learn what employees are griping about and how they view their companies, their industries, and their management teams.

As you can imagine, such information can be vital to shaping your approach to a job search and your emphasis in a résumé or during an interview. As with anything on the Web, however, remember: This is totally unfiltered; don't take anything at face value.

You can also use the Web as a direct job search tool. Huge databases such as Monster.com will store your résumé, even help you write an electronic version, and then make it available to web-surfing employers. While there remains considerable debate about how many jobs are filled online and in what functional areas, few people doubt that the numbers will increase substantially as years go by. The companies are there, the recruiters are there, the databases are there, and, increasingly, the job seekers are arriving.

So you need to be there.

Besides, in an increasingly technological world, what better way is there to demonstrate that you're a hip, with-it kind of candidate, that you can Unix, html, and cookie with the best of them?

For some time, I've been recommending that career-minded folks create a personal website as a repository for all their career management resources: résumé, work samples, log of personal and Web experience, links to professional and business websites, contact information. From this base, you can print out paper résumés, e-mail electronic versions to whomever you wish, and provide interested employers with a road map to your experience and knowledge.

And it's getting easier to do all the time. Most Internet gateways offer free Web space, as do web-hosting services such as GeoCities. Getting a domain name is dirt cheap. And the hosting sites even offer instruction and templates to help the technologically challenged set up a rudimentary web page. Many of the pages launched aren't exactly career builders. One former Netscape star used his to fire pot-shots at his former employer. On several I browsed, career development aspects took a backseat to personal passions, such as family and hobbies. I have yet to see one that fully taps the Internet's potential for career management and professional development, but people are starting to get a clue.

Bob Rindner, a Boca Raton, Florida, stockbroker, created an electronic résumé and placed it on a website that helps him job hunt and expand his network of contacts. He routinely refers contacts to the site, where they can study his résumé and click on embedded links to get more information.

On Mr. Rindner's website, for example, a reader can click on highlights that will link him or her to sites that explain brokerage concepts Mr. Rindner espouses. The hyperlinks could also connect to samples of your work, thus creating an electronic portfolio that doesn't clutter up the basic document.

The website also makes Mr. Rindner instantly accessible to people worldwide. This has led to consulting assignments from as far away as Tulsa, Oklahoma—jobs he might not otherwise have known about.

Robert M. Kaye has a personal web page that shows well the wide range of background information that should be on such sites. Mr. Kaye, formerly the executive project manager for data integration at DaimlerChrysler, has sections on his website for organizations and associations he belongs to, recent business seminars attended, and business books and trade periodicals he has read. He is explicit about his accomplishments. For instance, he discusses in detail the $8.2 million annual cost savings he got for one employer by installing new software.

Eventually, Mr. Kaye wants to add more sections: one that would chronicle advice, stories, and tactics he has picked up in his career, another offering advice for business travelers, and another linking to "outstanding employees and consultants I have worked with."

At Trev Hall's site, a natty-looking fellow in a long-sleeve yellow shirt and tie stares out at you. Okay, we can see there are no horns or open sores. What else can we learn? Do you want to know his work history? Click on his résumé. Want to know what he thinks about business and technology issues? Click on his essay section. Impressed? Want to talk to the man? Click on the pager icon and leave a message, or click on "Contact Trev" and fill out the e-mail form that pops up on screen.

Mr. Hall, president of the MBA class of 1999 at West Virginia University, Morgantown, made it easier for potential employers to learn about him, his history, his training, and even his personal life. It's all there on his website. You get a more rounded picture of him as a manager than you would normally get from reading a résumé. He also saw it as a way to reinvent himself as a jazzy, Internet-marketing kind of guy, something you wouldn't necessarily get from his previous experience as a customer service manager for Tenneco Packaging Co. in Pittsburgh.

"It gives you a competitive advantage," he says.

The essay section, covering such topics as quality control, management, and technology, is a great idea. The essays enable him to show off his knowledge on a variety of critical management issues. He then gets down to business in a section titled "Who Is Trev Hall and What Can He Do for Your Company?"

Mr. Hall launched a "résumé newsletter" to fill in some of the gaps on his site. Recently, he added a guestbook and, for those who don't sign in, a tracking icon that tells him who has visited the site. Both are useful tools for expanding his contact base.

Mr. Hall says he has gotten positive feedback from employers. "They say they've learned a lot about me without even talking to me," he says. The CEO of a local high-tech consortium clicked on the site after receiving an e-mail from Mr. Hall and soon called to offer a consulting assignment.

As personal websites grow in number, they should organize into communities of like interests. Mr. Hall and his classmates want to form an on-line alumni networking community that can share business ideas as well as opportunities.

Isn't that what the Internet is all about?

On-line Résumé (derivative of "Résumé"): An easy-to-access electronic document that potential employers can use to learn a lot about you, for better or worse.

4

How to tell good schmoozing
from bad

I once started out a column with this provocative quote from Bill
Morin, one of the pioneers of the outplacement industry: "Networking is dead."

You'd have thought I had just accused the president of being an
adulterer (okay, bad example). Anyway, the outpouring of shock and
dismay from the career guidance community was swift. Articles were
written to refute my alleged thesis. Letters to the editor excoriated
me. "Good networking will never die," proclaimed one of the kinder
correspondents.

If only they'd read the rest of the column.

I went on to say this—in the next paragraph, as a matter of fact:
"Before you start writing those letters, I know that networking
remains the No. 1 cause of job attainment and so does Mr. Morin.
He's just trying to be a bit provocative, and what could be more
provocative than dissing networking, the most sanctified, inviolate
staple of the job-search toolbox?"

Mr. Morin was trying to point out that networking has become so
pervasive, so overused, and, in some cases, so annoying that a backlash
was forming. "I know I'm saying something blasphemous," Mr.

Morin said. "But we have candidates saying, 'I called Joe, I called Marian, but they haven't called me back.'"

You know the networking drill. Call that engineer you met at the seminar, the consultant who did a project for you last year, your doctor, your lawyer, your Indian chief. Ask for job leads and get more names and call those people, building a pyramid of contacts. Arrange "informational interviews," wherein you ask people who might have job leads about everything except job leads (for instance, industry conditions, what their job is like, how's the weather, etc., etc.).

And get ready to be really frustrated.

Bob Hawkings knows all about it. Mr. Hawkings, a design engineer in Hayward, California, was out of work after Raychem cut him loose in 1995. He then made more than two hundred networking calls. The result: One job lead that didn't pan out. "Everything you read says 80 percent of jobs come through networking," he says. "But it hasn't worked too well for me. People are willing to chitchat, but they just don't have job leads."

Of course, much of this frustration surfaced during the the mid-1990s, the age of downsizing and huge layoffs. It slacked off during the dotcom rage, when so many companies were short of talent that they were sending out networking search parties for candidates. Ah, but now, as the economy slows and big layoffs are again in the headlines, job seekers need to again think of how to network wisely.

In the past decade, through good times and bad, one thing hasn't changed: Managers are harried, hassled, and just plain busy. They barely have time to deal with their own job openings, let alone act as advance scouts for job seekers they barely know. "Networking is a bankrupt concept," says Michael E. McGill, an organizational behavior expert who formerly chaired that department at the Southern Methodist University business school. Mr. McGill, over the years, has been besieged by networkers, some of whom he doesn't even know. "Out of every twenty people who call, I may talk to one person, and it's someone I have a real relationship with," he says.

At one point, Mr. Morin was getting about one hundred calls a week from job seekers, which is somewhat like the hypochondriac who corners the doctor at a cocktail party. A lot of it, he says, is "really far-out stuff. People I haven't seen in years, old neighbors I was never close to, people who know someone who knows me. My secretary grinds under the load, and I'm in the business. The average person at Pepsi-Cola doesn't want to deal with that."

"People are just stretched beyond belief," says David B. Opton, executive director of Exec-U-Net, a networking cooperative for senior executives. "You get a call at work that feels like networking, you want to throw up."

And if people feel too busy to answer phone calls, even fewer are willing to carve out time for informational interviews.

There are ways to take some of the load off your dialing finger during a job search. Internet databases, discussion groups, and e-mail lists provide a somewhat less painful way to make contacts. Networking newsletters like Exec-U-Net and NetShare provide another option, a virtual community of contacts who often contribute job leads to the group. They're particularly useful for employed but nervous executives who don't have the time to launch an all-out networking assault and fear that their boss will get wind of their search and use it as an excuse for termination. NetShare's Dave Theobald says senior executives feel safer with the job-listing services, which are delivered to their homes and promise confidentiality. The newsletters offer to subscribers job leads that have been gleaned from companies, fellow executives, and recruiters, along with skill requirements and contacts.

The services generally win kudos from users but worry some executive recruiters who don't like advertising their searches. But for job seekers, the important advice about networking is to devote the time and commitment needed to build full-blown relationships, not just a Rolodex filled with casual contacts. Your network may thus be smaller than some, but it will be more select, built of people who really know you and won't view your telephone call as an intrusion. And if you do it right, it will be composed of real live decision makers who may have jobs to grant someday.

Also, respect other people's time. Susan RoAne, a San Francisco author and speaker who refers to herself as "the mingling maven," recalls her annoyance with a desperate networker who pleaded for "just fifteen minutes," even after being told it wasn't a good time.

Savvy networkers know that networking means more than calling only when you need something. It means staying in contact on a regular basis, building a relationship, not just asking for things, but offering help and advice as needed. It means meeting for lunch occasionally, just to catch up.

So when you finally do need some help, the people you call are friends, not just casual acquaintances. And when you're looking for a job, a few good friends will do you a lot more good than a thousand passing acquaintances.

Networking isn't about how many people you know, it's about how willing and effective the people you know can be in helping you when you need help.

5

SHHH! BE WARY WHILE YOU'RE JOB HUNTING; THE BOSS MAY BE LISTENING

Recruiters are skulking about with tempting offers of bonuses and stock options and cars and a heckuva lot more money. You know of several colleagues who have hit the mother lode by switching jobs. Who could blame you for wanting to sniff around and see what earthly riches might await you in some greener pasture?

Your boss, that's who.

Despite all the rhetoric of recent years about the change in attitude of employers—lifetime employment is no longer guaranteed, employees must take responsibility for managing their careers, yada yada—many still go nuclear when they find one of their top people soliciting offers from competitors. The new economy may have changed the economic realities, but it hasn't erased human beings' egos and desire for loyalty from their top lieutenants. And nobody likes to lose a talented executive to the competition.

Does this mean you shouldn't be looking as long as you're gainfully employed? This is a difficult issue for me. I'm a hard-liner on loyalty issues; call me old-fashioned, I think loyalty matters. And spending your time courting other job offers while drawing a check from someone who expects your full attention to his or her business needs doesn't sit right with me. But I also think it's a two-way street, and since companies aren't displaying much loyalty to you, the economic survival of you and your family obviously takes precedence.

You could always quit first and look later. But even if you could afford time off without a paycheck, the reality remains that people who are performing well in good jobs are more desirable to recruiters and employers than those who, well, aren't. It's just human nature to have a nagging concern about why someone with apparently solid credentials isn't already employed and kicking your butt.

So if you're looking to maximize your career potential, you're going to have your antennae out at all times for advancement opportunities, even while you're already working.

This bit of perfidy obviously troubles managers who want to do a good job but don't want to miss opportunities for new challenges and financial security. A nervous midwest health care executive once called me, insisting on anonymity and wondering how he could look around for better opportunities without creating an awkward situation with his current employer. Should he tell his boss he was looking? Would he then become an ineffective lame duck and end up leaving on bad terms, thus nullifying any possible future return? Also, he added, he believed a promotion was just around the corner. Should he just wait for that?

The answer: Look, but be careful. Don't bet your career on your employer being enlightened on the subject. Ask around, and listen. How do senior executives talk about departed managers? Have they ever rehired someone who left? How have they reacted when discovering someone's job search?

If you've decided on an undercover job search mission, be doubly cautious. There are many ways your cover can be blown. If you're listing your résumé with an on-line database, insist on anonymity. You never know who could be surfing there. Don't respond to anonymous classified ads, lest it be from your current employer or one of his or her business buddies. And talk only to people you trust implicitly; stories abound about recruiters who spilled the beans to an employer about his or her employee's job search in the hope of getting the assignment to find a replacement (and no, all my recruiter friends, I don't think that's the norm in your profession, so cool it with the angry e-mails).

When Chris Brown felt his career at a telecommunications company had stalled, he decided to look elsewhere. But he couldn't afford a long period of unemployment, so he hung on to his job and kept his search secret amid "an atmosphere of paranoia" at the company.

At first, it was fun being James Bond on a secret mission. But as time wore on and the risk of exposure grew greater, so did the emotional strain on his family and the guilt he felt about deceiving the company. Working got harder. "Once you cross a bridge, it's difficult to stay focused," he says.

But after writing down his goals for a prospective job search, he decided he was doing this for all the right reasons and got "very resolute." He wanted to get his career moving forward again. "I wasn't just looking for a raise or promotion," he says.

He then enlisted four friends in the industry to help. They inquired discreetly about possible job openings, keeping his identity secret unless the job offer was serious and he consented to be identified.

He avoided mass mailings of his résumé. The more you spray your name around, the more likely you are to be discovered. He even avoided making inquiries at local trade meetings; too risky, he felt.

Make sure all responses to your inquiries are directed to your home or a separate, nonbusiness e-mail address. Plan absences from work before you start your job search, so that co-workers won't become suspicious if you're absent for job interviews. As Chicago-based recruiter Russ Riendeau puts it: "You see these employees who make it in even when the weatherman can't, and all of a sudden, they have to go to the foot doctor."

All this means your job search will probably take longer, and that can be frustrating. But if you're careful, it can all work out. Mr. Brown managed to keep his secret and eventually landed a good job as senior vice president of international sales for a Houston-based company.

A final thought: Both to allay suspicion and for your own peace of mind, be sure you don't give short shrift to your current job.

That means working even harder—and smarter—than usual. That means not arranging business trips so your employer can unwittingly pay your expenses for a job interview. It means using your home phone to make long-distance calls to prospective employers. It even pays to set up a separate job search phone line at home. That way, your boss or colleagues can't accidentally intercept a call from a suitor, and you won't miss calls because your teenager has the line tied up all day.

Keep your job-hunting antennae up even if you aren't really looking, but practice extreme discretion when you really are looking.

6

WHO GETS THE JOB, THE SPECIALIST OR THE GENERALIST?

Jacob Arbitman started with an undergraduate business degree and a graduate degree in organizational psychology. He stirred in brief stints as a financial analyst and with a start-up company overseas and figured he had a perfect recipe for a business development job with a consulting, venture capital, or mergers and acquisitions firm.

"To my surprise, the rest of the world still wants narrowly focused experts with familiar, cookie-cutter credentials," he says. "I was getting positive feedback, but a lot of people were puzzled about what to do with me."

So it goes in the never-ending war between specialists and generalists. Much of today's conventional wisdom stresses the importance of developing a view of the "big picture" and taking on a variety of assignments to pick up different skills. And those are useful perspectives for overall career advancement, especially after you've established yourself as a rising star and are looking around for new challenges to add to your résumé.

Unfortunately, most companies aren't going out and drafting the best athletes; they're focusing on their particular needs and the people who have the specific skills and track record to meet those needs.

This apparent contradiction has led to a pool of job market misfits who have slipped through the cracks of the new economy.

Martin Kantor fired off résumés stressing his finance and law degrees to companies offering financial management and legal positions. He got few responses. "I looked through the ads in the newspapers and they were usually pretty specific about experience," he says.

He was underqualified for management jobs and overqualified for entry-level jobs. For more than three years, he dabbled at odd jobs: technical support specialist, income tax preparer, stockbroker, and accounting software consultant. "Neither law firms nor businesses seemed the slightest bit interested in me," he says.

Messrs. Arbitman and Kantor needed to fine-tune their job search focus and reinvent themselves. Easier said than done.

Mr. Kantor rewrote his résumé to emphasize the computer-related skills he'd learned in classes and picked up on his own and eventually was hired by a small software company as a computer programmer.

Mr. Arbitman took a relatively low-paying financial analyst's job to sharpen his skills and knowledge. When he learned that many employers were seeking hires with certain graduate degrees, he returned to school. "I needed to retool myself and upgrade my credentials," he says. "People weren't going to pay me for being a well-rounded guy."

He finally landed a job he considered meaningful with a Deloitte & Touche group serving smaller firms. "All the consulting firms have budding practices for smaller firms," he says. "As they look at that market, they need people with broader skills."

So what can we learn from this?

As always, do your homework and customize your approach to fit companies' specific needs. Mr. Kantor found a match with a software firm when he stressed his computer skills.

If need be, go back to school to learn more targeted skills or take a step back in terms of pay and responsibility in order to gain needed skills.

There are places more likely to hire generalists. That's where your homework comes in. Mr. Arbitman found a consulting group that needed diverse skills to serve its small-business clientele.

Those small businesses are also likely candidates. Smaller companies are more likely to need people with broader skills, since their employees frequently must fill multiple roles.

Also look for companies in the midst of restructuring. In those organizations, job descriptions get scrambled, job functions get lumped together, and people with more diverse backgrounds may fit nicely.

You have more skills and abilities than you think, and there is almost certainly a company out there that really wants one of those skills or abilities.

7

ACING THE INTERVIEW

No company will hire you as a manager based solely on a spiffy résumé. Nor will sparkling references alone do the trick. Managers want to look you in the eye—or, more accurately, see if you look them in the eye. They want to know what you're like, how you handle yourself under pressure, and whether you're going to fit in or be a royal pain in the behind.

So to get the job, you've got to ace the interview.

Face it, plum jobs don't always go to the most skilled and knowledgeable. The workplace isn't a perfect meritocracy, not even in today's idealistic high-tech organizations. No matter how many degrees or promotions you've earned, you won't get that dream job if the interviewer across the table doesn't feel all warm and fuzzy about you. Hey, there are always others with equally sparkling backgrounds.

Besides, if credentials got you the job, interviews wouldn't be needed. It doesn't take long to confirm your qualifications; the rest of the time is spent assessing that squishy-soft, hard-to-measure stuff: your personality and style and how you handle tough issues. Those are the qualities that most often lead to job failure among executives; and companies are becoming more and more careful about them, because a bad hire at that level can be expensive.

Clearly, the interview is the most critical part of the job-hunting process. Theories on interviews—both giving and taking—abound. Some interviewers approach it as an adversarial situation, seeking to put the candidate under intense pressure and waiting to see if he or she will buckle. At many high-tech firms, interviews turn into Mensa entrance exams, replete with bizarre brainteasers meant to measure the job seeker's candlepower. At a conference a few years back, an investment banking recruiter told of an interview early in his career when a manager brought him into his office, then spent fifteen minutes reading the newspaper. At last he folded it up and ushered the young man out.

"What about the interview?" asked the befuddled youth.

"You had it," the interviewer said. "If you didn't have the nerve to interrupt me and demand your time, you don't belong in this business."

Experts contend that managers unconsciously form indelible opinions on the candidate's suitability early in the interview (I've heard estimates ranging from thirty seconds to five minutes). While managers certainly form early impressions that can affect the outcome of the interview, I doubt whether most actually make up their minds that quickly. Still, you don't have long to make a positive impression. An averted glance, a dead-fish handshake, a nervous giggle, and you're dead meat. I recall one candidate for a reporting job who spent the first ten minutes of our interview staring at his wringing hands. It was hardly a confidence builder, and he didn't get the job. The good news is, such afflictions aren't fatal. You can get better. That candidate did, and he was later hired and had a successful stint at the paper.

There are numerous keys to successful interviews. "Never let them see you sweat" is an old saw and still true. You want to exude confidence without spilling over into arrogance, a delicate balance. More than anything, though, managers want to believe that getting this job will make your decade. It's critical, particularly in the high-tech field, where managers are looking for people who want to "change the world," a refrain heard often in the halls of companies like Microsoft and the dotcomaniacs. Again, though, it's a balancing act; you must exhibit enthusiasm without getting creepy about it.

Also, you should never—I repeat, never—go into an interview without researching the company as if it were a critical classroom assignment. Rare is the company that doesn't believe its mission is critical to the survival of civilization as we know it. Anyone seeking work there should know that, too, they reason. So you must know the challenges it faces in producing and marketing its products or services, and the requirements of the work you would be doing should you be fortunate enough to get the job. You should be able to explain how the wondrous things you've accomplished in the past will help you soar like an eagle in your new assignment. (Here's where you weave in your past accomplishments, in an anecdotal tapestry that will clearly indicate why those experiences will enable you to excel in this new position.)

And in this potential new home, seldom—make that never—is heard a discouraging word. If you've got grievances against past bosses or firmly held opinions on the inhumane nature of the corporate world, keep them to yourself. Negativity never won fair maiden nor killer job.

Among her contemporaries at the Tuck School of Business at Dartmouth University, Kate Ill was known as a "rock star interviewee." Nothing she has done since her 1994 graduation has dispelled the notion. In her career, she has gotten coveted internships, jobs, and business school acceptances in spite of what she calls lackluster credentials. It's all in the interview.

Her initial edge comes from her freshly scrubbed, all-American good looks. It's the kind of look that employers find familiar and comfortable on a deep, subconscious level. It's easy to envision her in an important job, something all interviewers try to do. Anyone who tells you that appearance doesn't matter in a job interview doesn't know what he's talking about—and probably looks like Brad Pitt to boot. Undercover experiments have persuasively demonstrated that when credentials are equal, the tall and slender routinely get the job over the short and chubby.

Obviously, though, not everyone swims in Ms. Ill's Scandinavian American gene pool. But you can at least make sure your appearance, if not an automatic advantage, isn't a disadvantage. You can be well groomed and well dressed. You don't have to be a slave to the dress-for-success gurus, but a baggy, wrinkled suit and dirty nails aren't going to win you many jobs, either.

Ms. Ill's demeanor also helps. She exudes easygoing confidence; she's direct and assertive, and she doesn't hesitate to crack a smile or use humor to put people at ease. "I'm good at talking to people," she says. "I don't get freaked out by interviews."

Make sure your answers are complete (you don't want to seem evasive) but concise. Overexplaining everything will mark you as a high-maintenance employee and a bore. What could be worse?

Finally, anticipate holes in your story and be prepared with answers that will put to rest your interviewer's concerns. "I look at my résumé and think a lot about what an interviewer might ask," Ms. Ill explains. "You have to have an explanation for every move in your life, why you made it, and what you got out of it. Then you have to spin it into what it would mean for them if they hire you."

In her interviews, Ms. Ill is confronted regularly with questions about her record and career choices. Why were her grades only average? Why did she choose to major in religion, and how would that help her in a business career? Why did she choose to work at a smaller investment banking firm after interning at giant Morgan Stanley, turning her back on a job coveted by most of her business school peers?

She crafted answers for each issue before going into her interviews:

On grades: "I said there were two ways to look at my grades—with my freshman year or without it."

On her major: Religion was one of the hardest majors in the school; it helped hone her critical thinking abilities and made her a more rounded person, she says. She felt it also marked her as a risk taker, a quality coveted by most companies. "If all I thought about was my GPA, I would never have majored in religion," she says.

On Morgan Stanley: Fortunately, she was able to say she was invited back by the investment banking firm; to be snubbed would have been a huge black mark. Nevertheless, she explained, the smaller, less structured firm allowed her broader authority and greater contact with top executives than she could get at the big firm.

The question arose when she interviewed with Alex. Brown in 1996. Knowing from her research that Alex. Brown had a respected high-tech group, she replied: "What I really want to focus on now is emerging growth and technology. I don't care about having IBM as a client. I want to work with cool companies who really need us."

As in all interviews, those explanations didn't fly with everyone. In real life, some people just don't buy your story. That's something else the gurus rarely tell you. Still, that can be a good thing, providing you with a sense of the company's attitudes and culture. Ms. Ill recalls a Goldman, Sachs recruiter who asked, during an interview for an internship, whether her decision to major in religion and thus risk a lower GPA wasn't shortsighted. "I would never want to work somewhere that wouldn't appreciate that," she decided.

As Ms. Ill demonstrates, the interview also provides a precious opportunity to take the temperature of the company, something many interviewees miss because they're so focused on their own performance. There's much to be learned from the person on the other side of the table. How do managers here interact with people? Is your prospective boss an insecure pipsqueak who will make your life miserable? Does she take an adversarial stance during interviews, which might indicate a hostile working environment? What traits and values does she focus on in her questions?

As Ms. Ill gained more experience in interviewing, she watched the interviewer more closely. "You think more about adapting your personality to the person across the table," she says. "If they're gregarious, you can be a little more gregarious. If they're shy, I'll be a little quieter; I don't want to intimidate them."

Her toughest move came in 1998. Tired of the outsider world of investment banking, she wanted to get inside the corporate world, where the big decisions are made. Software, she decided, was a promising industry, but one in which she had no experience.

By now, she had a track record in business, which meant fewer questions about grades and majors.

As usual, she wasn't dealing from a position of power. "This time," she says, "it was lack of specific industry experience."

To address that, you have to be honest about what you lack and address how you'll overcome that. And why, interviewers will want to know, are you abandoning the comfort of what you know for the uncertainty of what you don't know?

In this case, Ms. Ill explained that she wasn't going away from anything, that she was moving to software, which she saw as an industry with a promising future that would provide her with a new personal challenge.

One last bit of critical advice about interviewing: No matter how good you feel about the session, don't get pressured into immediately accepting an offer. In today's talent-short world, recruiters act like used-car salesmen, eager to close the deal before you leave the showroom.

But there is still much to learn about your prospective employer. There's all that pesky stuff about money and benefits, of course (more on that later), but there's also the critical people equations. Ms. Ill says she won't accept a job offer until she meets her prospective co-workers. "If I'm going to be working long hours with these people, I need to meet them," she says.

Half of acing an interview is knowing as much as you can about the company before the interview; anticipating what the company wants to know about you is the other half.

8

GETTING WHAT YOU'RE WORTH

Now that they've professed their undying love for you, you can finally talk to your future employer about the subject everyone is most interested in anyway—money.

Oh, I know it's considered déclassé to say so; of course, you're not in it for anything so crass. It's the challenge, the chance to excel.

Look, everyone wants a job that excites them, that truly is a challenge; that's a given. But they also want to get top dollar for it. As much as we hate to admit it, most of us do keep score, and we keep score in dollar signs.

So let's accept this dirty little secret and get down to the important job of getting what you're worth.

That has gotten somewhat easier, thanks to the explosion of salary information available on websites and in career and trade publications. Ten years ago, it was nearly impossible to glean such inside information. Companies kept a tight rein on salary data, figuring the less you knew, the less they would have to pay you. This created huge inequities. While many companies parceled out miserly annual salary bumps to current employees, pleading poverty, they frequently shoveled large sums at hotshots they were trying to lure from other companies, even if they were filling similar jobs and had similar backgrounds to those of folks already on the payroll.

As in everything else, knowledge is power. Of course, this kind of leverage is good only as long as the prospective employer is convinced that someone else will actually pay the princely sum you're demanding—and that they can't get someone as good as you for less. So you'd better be sure your demands are reasonable and that you truly deserve the raise you're seeking. The kind of leverage an Internet whiz had in the free-spending days of 1999, when everyone was hiring and talent was short, dropped precipitously in the down days of 2000, when companies were folding or axing workers by the barrelful.

Still, it never hurts to know what the going rate is.

So where to start? Major business publications publish annual pay surveys, as do most major professional groups. Cyberspace also contains considerable data, including Salary.com, WageWeb, SalaryExpert, JobStar, and career development sites such as Monster.com and Wet-Feet.com. There are many more from on-line publications and trade associations. Job search networks such as Exec-U-Net in Norwalk, Connecticut, and NetShare in San Francisco provide salary guidance to their subscribers through the hundreds of managerial job openings they list, most of which include salary information.

You can also cull salary information from seemingly unlikely sources. Liz Ryan, when she was a human resources executive for a major computer equipment maker, used to scan general-interest publications, from *Money* to *Glamour,* that profiled successful executives. The articles often included compensation information.

With all of these sources, be thorough and skeptical. Not all surveys are alike. Check the source for inherent biases. See how detailed the information is. National averages for broad, generic job categories won't help you much; if you're seeking a job in New York or Boise, Idaho, you need to know what the local going rate is. You must also factor in industry, company size, skills required, and, of course, demand. Most of the sky-high salaries reported for MBA holders, for instance, come from consulting and investment banking firms. "If you're not looking at those industries, you're not going to be paid as much," says Abigail Quackenbush, who left a large consulting firm in Atlanta and started a smaller one of her own in northern Virginia.

Ms. Quackenbush's own pay dilemma: Could she earn more by jumping to another consulting firm or by starting her own firm?

She scoured Search Bulletin for available jobs and salaries. She contacted her alma mater, Northwestern's Kellogg Business School, to see what recruiters were offering on campus. She also tapped into the school's alumni network for contacts she could quiz.

Some people stonewalled her, but most would at least talk about their benefits package, if not their pay. Those considering their own "career transitions" were more open, Ms. Quackenbush found. Revealing pay is still taboo, but most people will at least discuss salary ranges.

Ms. Quackenbush also tested the market for her own company by taking on some consulting assignments. She eventually identified a market niche (midsize, high-growth companies) that wasn't being served adequately and decided she could make more money starting her own firm, Cornerstone Group.

If you're thinking of moving from a large company to a smaller one, contact people in venture capital associations who might know about salaries at companies they've backed, or the Association for Corporate Growth, a group for individuals working in middle-market corporate growth, corporate development, or mergers and acquisitions.

Executive recruiters are good barometers of demand: if they're calling you daily, you're in a field hot enough to warrant a premium over survey figures. If they blow you off like so much lint, you're chilly. And don't look just at job titles. Match up your skills and experience levels with what the company is seeking. Titles can mean different things in different places. In recent years, many workers have added extra responsibilities without changing job titles. Brent Longnecker recalls that in one executive job at a big accounting firm, he wound up doing the jobs of four people but didn't get paid any more. He eventually left for another major audit firm.

But before you rush out to claim every dollar you're worth, Mr. Longnecker cautions, remember that there is value also in the right corporate culture. He asks: "Is it worth it to move from a creative environment where you have a lot of autonomy to one where you're going to make $3,000 more a year, but people are going to tell you what to do?"

Unfortunately, that answer all too often is yes. It gets in the way of good decisions. When I read some of the advice offered by career experts, for example, I just shake my head. They advise you to negotiate every tidbit, from salary to vacation to profit-sharing terms to health insurance terms to the configuration of your office space.

It is not always wise.

First of all, companies often have these policies etched in stone and wouldn't negotiate them unless you were the second coming of Jack Welch. But even if they could, they wouldn't enjoy it much, and that would cast a shadow over you. Nobody wants to hire a jailhouse lawyer who's going to haggle over every little detail. Put yourself in the hiring manager's shoes. Would you want to hire a pain in the butt like you?

So before you go in, decide the issues that are really important to you and focus on them. Be resolute but reasonable. Have a "Plan B" when negotiating your major points. An example: If the salary offered is less than you'd like but still somewhere in the ballpark, see if you can negotiate an accelerated performance review schedule, with some specific performance measurements that would trigger the increases that would get you where you want to be. Companies may be more willing to pay your price after you've proven that you can deliver the goods.

Whatever you do, don't make the first offer; that's one bit of conventional wisdom that still holds true. If the company won't go first, politely express your deep and abiding interest in the job and your hope that they'll contact you soon when they've decided what they want to pay.

Once you do get an offer, don't respond immediately, whether you feel it's high, low, or right on target. Tell them you'd like twenty-four hours to study the offer. That gives you a chance to recheck your research and to carefully consider your response after your initial emotional reaction has passed.

Finally, be reasonable and flexible. Don't let your ego get in the way of a great opportunity by being too rigid and demanding on salary terms. Fair is good enough.

Getting what you're worth means knowing what you're worth in the current market, and that takes a blend of skepticism, research, and self-knowledge.

PART TWO

GETTING AHEAD

9

TAKING THE ROAD LESS TRAVELED

Let's say you're starting out your corporate career without the sparkling credentials that favor some of your peers. You didn't graduate magna cum lordy from some Ivy League school or pick up an MBA from Wharton or Stanford. Your name isn't automatically tossed into the hopper for plum assignments.

Just how do you get ahead?

Look for the dirty work, the stuff nobody else wants to do. It's a formula that worked for Joe Booker. Throughout his career, he has often been the youngest and most inexperienced guy in his department. He frequently faced situations where he wasn't properly trained for his job. And sometimes he was the only African American on the job.

So he wasn't often handed the high-profile, big-ticket job upon which fast trackers typically built their careers.

Which was just fine with him. If he could take on the dirty jobs nobody else wanted and do them well, he figured he would turn some heads. "Some of them were risky jobs," he acknowledges, "but if you succeeded, the payoff was high."

It certainly worked for Mr. Booker, who is currently vice president of operations for Alteon Systems, a computer networking company, the latest in a string of high-profile Silicon Valley posts.

Mr. Booker's career strategy started to take shape when he was a young electronics specialist on his first assignment at the predominantly white Keesler Air Force Base. Reasoning that a plum assignment wasn't likely, he inquired into the job considered the most thankless at the base. That, he learned, was Doppler radar, an assignment shunned by many because of the complexity of the equipment. When he mastered the equipment, he quickly became a star at the base. He learned a valuable lesson: Asking for and then excelling at thankless tasks earns you considerable respect and admiration. "It really opened doors," he says.

At IBM, after leaving the air force, he opted to start in the less glamorous field of manufacturing because there was less competition and the results he achieved there would be measurable—and thus irrefutable.

He later moved to Memorex, following a boss who promised to make him a manager. But his strategy for advancement remained the same. At weekly production meetings, he volunteered for jobs that were behind schedule or involved introducing a new product into a tough market. "If people were saying, 'This is something we can't do,' I'd say, 'I'll do it.'"

Working against the odds forced him to become resourceful and taught him the importance of forging alliances. Once, he bet his boss he could meet a seemingly impossible deadline for introducing a new disk drive. To win the bet, he had to overcome a history of interdepartmental political hassles that had plagued the project. So he concentrated on developing a close relationship with an engineering project manager whose team was crucial to the project's success. He won the bet (his boss had to bake him a cake).

Be forewarned, however: This is a path for the overlooked and the overachiever. You must constantly overcome negative first impressions based solely on your background. And on this less-than-perfect orb, it isn't always a smooth path, where the righteous and just are rewarded. To succeed requires more self-analysis and self-improvement than your more credentialed colleagues. Mr. Booker got in the habit of delivering his own bruising review each year. "When you do a job well, ask yourself, 'How do I expand?'" he says. "'What skills do I need to take this next step?'" So, for example, he took finance classes to help him run a factory better.

Still, the climb hasn't been straight uphill, another risk of this back-door career strategy. He started his own company, merged it with another, and served as president of the combined entity. But he clashed with the board over strategy and left. Later, he agreed to be CEO of another company but stepped aside when a potential CEO with a life-giving capital infusion came along.

But let's have a reality check here: it isn't necessary to be CEO to have a successful career. To remind him of this, Mr. Booker created a list of his job requirements: a job where he could be successful, with co-workers he enjoyed; a company that would make money; a growing experience so he wouldn't be bored; and an executive position. "It didn't say I had to be CEO," he noted after completing the list.

Still, his willingness to risk all on unglamorous and difficult jobs has paid off with a highly successful executive career by anyone's standards. And for managers with less than A+ credentials, that isn't a bad template to emulate.

It won't be easy, but you can overcome obstacles in your career path by taking risky or dirty jobs nobody else wants and doing them well.

10

HUNTING THE ELUSIVE MENTOR

The question I've been asked most frequently over the years—usually in a tone of utter frustration—is this: How can I find a mentor?

It is one of the oldest and truest axioms of career management: If you are to reach great heights in corporate America, someday, somehow, someone is going to have to wrap a warm and sheltering arm around your shoulder and guide you through the rocky shoals of office politics, unwritten rules, and management idiosyncrasies. That person, of course, is the mentor, one of a dying breed of senior managers who give willingly of themselves to guide the career of a budding star.

This is, of course, a good thing. How could it not be? Everyone needs that sage veteran adviser who's been through the wars, knows the ropes, knows where the bodies are buried . . . sorry, can't think of any more clichés just now. And everyone needs a powerful advocate, someone who sits with the high council behind closed doors when promotions are being pondered and tosses your name into the pot with gushing praise.

So why are these birds becoming so rare? Time and constancy have become factors. People work such long hours in such intense environments these days, they have little time or energy for mentoring.

Further, with fewer executives staying with one company for extended periods, mentoring relationships are difficult to sustain. You snag a bigwig as a mentor and six months later . . . whoops, there he goes, off to another division or, worse, another company. Years of corporate turmoil—mergers, restructurings, downsizings, delayerings, cross-training—have also muddied the waters, moving people around like rats in a maze and making extended mentoring relationships difficult. Women and minorities have a particularly tough time, because their choices are limited.

In truth, though, this mentoring thing has always been problematic. The sad fact is, many people just can't be bothered. Most of the successful executives studied in the 1988 book *The Lessons of Experience,* written by three researchers from the Center for Creative Leadership (CCL), listed their exposure to mentoring as "rare or nonexistent." And those relationships that did form rarely lasted longer than three years.

Whatever the reason, companies and individuals have had to become more flexible and creative about the concept of mentoring. First of all, forget the idea of a single, all-knowing person who will advise you, guide you, and be your advocate for life. That isn't impossible, but it isn't likely.

Instead, think of forming your own board of advisers, a kind of corporate board of directors for you. For her board, Debra Facktor draws candidates from both inside and outside her company and shuffles the composition from time to time, depending upon her career needs. "At one stage of your career, it may be advantageous to have an aggressive male mentor," says Ms. Facktor, chief of Moscow operations for ANSER Center for International Space Cooperation, a nonprofit research firm in Arlington, Virginia. "At another stage, you may want a woman who has been through the experience of balancing family and a career."

Happy hunting grounds for mentors outside your immediate company include alumni groups, professional societies, and community groups. Former company executives are good candidates, says John Chung, a director of risk management for American Express's consumer card services group, who meets frequently with a former company VP for lunch or golf. If you can't find readily available mentors, you might even consider springing for a professional coach, just to have a sounding board.

Cherie Gary, a regional public relations manager for AT&T Wireless in Dallas, recommends scouring the halls for middle managers as well as senior managers. "Look for someone who has been kicked around the block a few more times than you and can alert you to pitfalls ahead," she says.

One strength of the board concept is that it provides you with a variety of mentors with different areas of expertise and personalities as well as different management styles. "Different kinds of people have different things to teach," says Kathleen R. C. Gisser, a research scientist for Eastman Kodak. "It's especially important not to 'double your losses' by always choosing mentors that have personalities similar to your own."

Ms. Gary says that one of her most influential mentors was a demanding male manager with whom she had little in common. She credits him with teaching her a work ethic and networking skills. "He was the one who taught me, 'No matter how tired you are, go,'" she says.

Developing a relationship with a mentor is all about forging common bonds, so it wouldn't hurt to learn some of the target's favorite things. Lita Alessandra, manager of worldwide financial benefits for Texas Instruments, notes that she bonded with one mentor over a shared interest in running.

To get the most out of a mentoring relationship, look for managers you'd like to emulate, both in business savvy and in operating style. And be sure it's someone you trust enough to talk about touchy issues.

Ms. Gisser says her best mentors didn't just give quick answers to questions, but helped her think through problems. Also, she advises, look for mentors who will share their failures as well as their successes. "Some of the most important things good mentors can teach are how they have recovered from their own setbacks and failures," Ms. Gisser says.

Knowing what you want from a mentor can also save time. When paired with her mentor in a formal, company-engineered mentoring program, Ms. Alessandra compiled a list of areas she thought the mentor could help with, including conflict resolution and running a large organization. "I'd like to grow professionally, and I've identified skills I'd like to improve," she says.

It helps if you can take your mentoring in small doses and not wear out your welcome. It can be frightening to be someone's mentor and thus take some responsibility for their career. But it's less intimidating if you're just someone who occasionally seeks advice on specific topics. With a limited investment of time, the mentor won't feel so put upon.

Finally, there are dangers to being someone's protégé. Consider executive recruiter Brad Hoffman's experience as a Procter & Gamble sales manager: When his fourteen-year career there stalled, his mentors "were so busy trying to save their own careers that they gave me no help at all," he says. "One of them was out of favor, and my relationship with him actually hurt me—guilt by association."

Indeed, the CCL researchers traced the downfall of some executives to overdependence on a mentor. "You have to watch out for the label 'So-and-so Junior,' which tends to brand you as incapable of independent thought," says Christopher Doyle, director of fuel and asset management for Gas Energy Inc. in Brooklyn, New York. Mr. Doyle believes his layoff from a former employer was engineered by a vindictive former mentor. "If a mentor sees you as a threat to his own job security, you can spend a great deal of time pulling knives out of your back," he says.

Another good reason for having a board of mentors. Then you can all watch each other's backs.

Real mentors are rare, so create your own board of advisers. Look for advice and encouragement among a variety of people senior to you, including people very different from you.

11

BEING A HUB: LEADING WHEN
YOU'RE NOT THE LEADER

Gayle Crowell sweeps into the room like a latter-day Loretta Young, purposefully, confidently, and stylishly. Her hair is perfectly coiffed. She is clad in a fashionable black dress with a long, matching piece that swoops around her neck and back over her shoulders like wings.

No wonder her PR agency put together a CEO-as-supermodel promotional package for her, complete with a portfolio of glamour shots suitable for *Elle.* Ms. Crowell, who professes embarrassment at the glamour hype, exudes presence. And that presence has everything to do with her career success. She used it to become a hub of organizational activity and influence wherever she worked, even in situations where she didn't have official power and title. For people like Ms. Crowell, with high levels of confidence and a winning way with people, being a corporate hub is a surefire road to upper management.

How do you become one? By being decisive, showing initiative, gaining credibility by developing a broad range of expertise, cultivating key relationships, and especially, positioning yourself as a broker of people and ideas. In any corporate setting, there are always one or more hubs. They're the ones others seek out when they need information, a sounding board, a sympathetic ear, or help influencing others. I've known several hubs in my career; they tend to be charming, charismatic, ambitious, and extremely adept politically. And they almost always rise rapidly in the organization.

Ms. Crowell's rapid rise began in Carson City, Nevada, where the elementary school teacher garnered considerable publicity by buzzing around the state in a private plane to dun CEOs for funds to buy computers and software for students. Her campaign also attracted the attention of Cubix, a local high-tech company that recruited her ardently. Knowing little about the company's technology or the requirements of the undefined job she was being offered, she initially said no. "They could have made me janitor," she says. But the company persisted, testing her belief that too many women fall short in their careers because they are afraid to take career-altering risks. Besides, here was someone offering her four times her teacher's salary to work with her beloved computers. She took the job in 1984.

Her first assignment: Prepare a report on how the company should proceed in 4GL technology. (For the technology challenged, that means fourth-generation programming language.) "I didn't know what 2GL or 3GL was," she recalls. But she read everything she could find on the subject, pumped managers at other companies for information, and eventually produced an extensive report, complete with recommendations on how the company should change its current approach to the technology and with whom it should develop partnerships.

She pulled it off, she believes, because she is very analytical, obsessive about learning, and determined to prove herself. She soon became the company's ace troubleshooter, sent in to run a software testing department, to set up a telemarketing operation, to study the potential of a new market. In each assignment, she went in without the benefit of a senior executive's title or a clear line of authority. But it was becoming clear she had influence with senior management.

Ms. Crowell touts teaching as a great training ground for hub aspirants. "You have to command the attention of thirty-five, fifty, or a hundred people" of all different stripes, she explains. Good teachers learn to inspire, communicate, listen, and understand—just the qualities many companies say they want in their top executives these days.

At Cubix, she struggled early on to find her role. So she asked to meet with customers. "I really tried to pull customers out, learn about their business," she says. "How can we add value to that business?" Her experience as a troubleshooter at Cubix, encompassing nearly every department in four years, was the equivalent of getting an MBA, she says. That's why she's a big fan of smaller companies for learning the ropes. Big companies tend to funnel people into narrow functional areas. But in a smaller company you frequently cross departmental boundaries. "If you want to learn about finance, you can just hang out with the CFO," she says.

At Cubix, she also learned that commanding respect and allegiance had little to do with commanding. "Instead of asking people, 'Would you do this?'" Ms. Crowell explains, "I'd say, 'How can I help you?' If I did help you, eventually, you would help me."

As her reputation and knowledge increased, Ms. Crowell discovered that her role as a hub enabled her to develop close relationships with those in power. "It's a fine line," she says. "You could also be seen as a brown-noser or a powermonger."

To keep that from happening, she learned an important lesson: If you increase your boss's influence, you usually increase your own. (Yes, I know there are credit hogs out there who steal your best ideas and keep you out of the limelight. But they aren't the majority. For tips on handling those jerks, refer to the chapters on bad bosses and office politics.)

Ms. Crowell says she didn't have many problems with credit hogs. "You go to a person with power and say you're looking at, say, electronic business-to-business sales and you think it could be interesting for the company," she says. "You ask them, 'Would you like to hear more about it? Let me research it.' So I've made this person, who doesn't have the time to do this on his own, smarter." If the boss decides to go ahead with the proposal, she says, he can use her to build support for the plan with others.

In that example, she says, you're a rainmaker, because you're bringing in more business, and a hub, because you're leveraging your influence to promote ideas. "You can also be a sponsor of someone who would otherwise be transparent," she says. "Your endorsement, because you have tremendous credibility, can fuel their career."

Eventually, she was appointed national sales director for Cubix, despite having no sales experience. From there, she became director of North American sales for DSC, a switch maker; a group director at

Oracle; vice president of worldwide sales for Plexus, a unit of Recognition International; general manager of high-tech start-up ViewStar; and in 1998, chairman, president, and CEO of RightPoint Inc. She managed to turn around the struggling Silicon Valley software company, which was then sold to E.piphany.

Her abilities as a hub were put to a stern test at Oracle, where she was brought in to convince an organization built on direct sales of the need to sell through other retail channels as well. In a company where salespeople are trained to be take-no-prisoner "Oracle Animals," that didn't sit well. Even CEO Lawrence Ellison, the original Oracle Animal, was hard to sway, she says. "I was not a high executive, I was just below the vice president level," she says. "I had to sell all the VPs, Larry, and Mike [then president Mike Fields] on why this was a good thing for the organization."

Nothing short of a cultural makeover was needed. So she built a business case, analyzing the market and Oracle's position, where the market was headed, and why the company must change. She identified the barriers to that change: a compensation system that didn't reward people for selling to resellers, a training process that strongly emphasized direct sales, and a corporate attitude that emphasized winning over developing partnerships.

Then she took her ideas door-to-door at the company. "If I'd get one person's support, I'd use that to sell the next one," she says. "It was like a political process."

That again involved serving as a broker for each side. She had to coach the resellers on how to curry favor with company salespeople. "I'd tell them, 'Look, the direct guy won't just give you all his deals,'" she recalls. "'Bring him some deals, then he'll bring you some.'" And she had to convince salespeople that dealing with their onetime foes could be beneficial.

Later, when she was brought in as general manager of ViewStar, a foundering start-up, Ms. Crowell says one of her first tasks was to identify the company's floor leaders and sell them on the drastic steps needed to right the ship, including axing half the employees. The three women she singled out were "instrumental in carrying my message and explaining the bad news," she says, a chore that would have been near impossible for an outsider.

"The smartest thing a CEO can do is to recognize early who the floor leaders are, because they are so effective at influencing the people in the organization," she says.

Bringing together diverse people or presenting new or untested ideas within a company can make you a power broker even if you don't have a power broker's title.

12

Is that promotion right for you?

Forget about all those books on how to make a dramatic career change or *50 Ways to Leave Your Lover or Employer*. Instead, let's talk about the more commonplace but all-important career decisions you must make within your current organization: Should you take an offered promotion or pursue a vacant position—or should you take a pass?

Maybe it's not the stuff of best-sellers (although I fervently hope it is), but it's the meat and potatoes of most people's careers. And by most accounts, it's getting more complex and dicey as organizations grow willy-nilly, thus pushing people to stretch to fill unfilled jobs—or conversely, as they shrink, flatten, and restructure, rendering career ladders unrecognizable.

But for the most part, the old rules of engagement still pertain: Know thyself, do your homework, and look before you leap. There, I've filled my quota of clichés for this chapter.

While I'm all in favor of stretch assignments, you don't want one that will leave ugly stretch marks. Your bosses don't always know what's best for your career and in some cases may even be setting you up to fail (who have you pissed off lately?). While a promotion may mean more authority, visibility, money, and opportunities for advancement, it won't help your career much if you're being hurled, unprepared, into a den of vipers or a position you can't reasonably master.

Of course, don't underestimate yourself, either. Corporate lore is filled with tales of seemingly unqualified people who excelled in jobs because they had strong analytical skills, worked well with people, and trusted a superior who sensed they had a knack for the job. General Electric is famous for jump-starting careers with these so-called stretch assignments.

That notwithstanding, the pressure to perform well—and to do it right out of the chute—is enormous these days; taking a promotion, then screwing up, may do more damage to your career than turning it down, especially if you put the right spin on your rejection speech.

There is considerable external and self-imposed pressure to accept a promotion, lest you be seen as unambitious, so spike that notion right away by talking about the kind of assignment you'd be eager to take on, an assignment where you feel you can make a bigger contribution to the company. Companies seem to be somewhat more understanding of this these days, particularly with the growth of concern over work-life balance.

David Woodard worried about that when he rejected an offer to manage the environmental, health, and safety group at Alza Corp.'s Vacaville, California, manufacturing facility. "My initial reaction was, 'I'm twenty-seven, this is my break, my one shot, I've got to do it,'" he says.

But for Mr. Woodard, an environmental engineer for the pharmaceutical company, it meant moving a hundred miles away from his girlfriend, who couldn't move, the abandonment of friends and a lifestyle he loved, and the postponement of an MBA program he felt would benefit him more in the long run.

Afterward, he said work was going great and he had completed two quarters of MBA work (another good way to demonstrate your continuing ambition). Both his current and would-be bosses have been supportive, he said, and he hasn't seen any indication that he is viewed in a lesser light.

Kathy Wilson learned the hard way to be cautious about accepting promotions. She landed a promotion to manager of a training group for a Norwest credit card services unit in Des Moines. But she soon discovered that a training manager must manage plus deliver services. After four and a half years, she tired of the eighty-hour weeks and relinquished the managerial part of her job.

Ms. Wilson says she won't know if this is a career limiting move unless she attempts to reenter management with Norwest, a move she isn't currently contemplating. "I was at a point where I was willing to take a risk to obtain some balance between my work and home life," she says.

Ms. Wilson's experience demonstrates the need to think carefully about what a promotion truly entails and what expectations your boss has about your performance. The newly minted manager frequently finds that she no longer has time for the job-related tasks she truly enjoys, that she needs a whole new set of skills, and that her relationship with friends has changed.

Before putting on your stern managerial face and toting that big paycheck home, talk to your current supervisor and others who have made similar moves to find out how managers spend their time and what skills are required for the new job. Ask what the company is expecting from you in the new assignment.

Darshan Shah, a chemical engineer and project manager with Eli Lilly, was seeking to reinvent his career. He first considered a seemingly exciting job as a department head. But after interviewing the person who was leaving the job—Why was he leaving? What did he like and not like about it?—he decided he didn't like his chances for success there.

Instead, he proposed the creation of a new job as a senior human resources associate. What about that job appealed to him? "It was a chance for me to be the benchmark for the job that others would follow," he says. Also, he thought the job required some of the same tools he used as a project manager—analyzing and selecting vendors, for example—and thus felt more comfortable.

Questions to ask include the shape the department's in, the future for the product or service provided, and the style and personality of those higher up in that department's pecking order. Just don't ask too many people for advice, Mr. Shah cautions. "You'll just get confused and won't be able to make a decision."

In the end, the decision is a highly individual one. Most promotions are good for you and shouldn't require much deliberation. But there are those times when you are being shipped to a job where you believe strongly you can't succeed—whether it's because you lack the skills or the department is on an irreversible downward spiral. In those cases, don't let your ego or the expectations of others force you into an unwise decision.

When a promotion is offered, don't leap at it headfirst. Saying no to a job you don't think is a good move for you will do less damage to your career than taking the job and botching it.

13

BREAKING OUT OF
YOUR PIGEONHOLE

Is your career stuck in neutral because someone has slapped a label on you that won't come off? It's called being pigeonholed, and Bob Bugiada provides a striking example.

Years ago, Mr. Bugiada, then an aerospace engineer, worried that the industry was headed for a steep decline. He decided to shift to the construction industry. But he kept being relegated to less prestigious government projects. He had been pigeonholed as an aerospace engineer with a government contracts mind-set. "That 'aerospace reject' label stuck to me like doggie doo," he recalls.

The problem manifests itself in a variety of ways. Some people become so proficient and indispensable at their jobs, their bosses connive to prevent their leaving. Some people are viewed as having limited skills and thus aren't considered for other opportunities. Others pigeonhole themselves, fearful that any other career direction would be too risky.

Ah, but take heart. There are ways to bust out.

First, some preventive medicine: Make sure you're not unknowingly climbing into a future pigeonhole. Had Mr. Bugiada studied his employer's corporate culture more closely before signing on, he would have known that the company didn't like to rotate assignments. He learned that painful lesson later, when he asked to rotate to sales and marketing to broaden his résumé and skills. His request was ignored.

Had he checked on the career paths of those in the company's government contracts business, he might also have learned of the company's preference for people who had private sector experience. He might have found the manager who later told him that "most aerospace people wash out of here." Instead, he discovered the bias during his first performance review, when his manager said he was doing well, "despite where he came from."

Mr. Bugiada addressed the problem head-on, going to his bosses and stating his disinclination to work on certain projects. Although they honored his request, it seems to me that he could just as easily have been labeled a whiner—hardly a career boost. Considering his earlier frustration, when his request for sales and marketing experience was ignored, he may have felt he had no other choice. But it would have been better in my view to put a more positive spin on the situation—explain that he felt he was being pigeonholed and that he would like the opportunity to prove them wrong. Then, he could list the types of projects he'd like a shot at, along with the reasons he feels he could excel in those jobs.

Sometimes, if the company won't provide opportunities for you to broaden your portfolio, you have to do it on your own.

After twenty years as a corporate manufacturing executive, Bernie Nagle wanted to shift into the business process improvement field. But he had little background in that relatively new discipline. He started by reading everything on the subject he could find and contacting the authors, asking them how he could learn more about their ideas. "You can't be bashful," he says. "You can't expect people to come to you." He strongly recommends attending seminars on the subjects that intrigue you, "even if you have to do it on your own nickel." He brainstormed with like-minded peers at professional society meetings, adapting the best ideas to situations in his department.

As his knowledge grew, he positioned himself as an expert by writing articles for trade publications and, eventually, a book, *Leveraging People and Profit: The Hard Work of Soft Management.*

He left his executive position to become a consultant on business process improvement, and sixteen months later, armed now with both knowledge and experience, he was hired by Berg Electronics, St. Louis, as director of global business process improvement. "You have to have the courage to re-create your own future," he says.

Another tip: Brush up on your presentation skills. A vice president at a health care company, who didn't want to be named, says most people who get pigeonholed are unable to "sell themselves internally." He suggests getting sales and marketing experience to sharpen your ability to present ideas to a group. "Careers are made in meetings and how you present yourself," he says.

What you say in casual conversation also counts. If you constantly talk just about your job, you're liable to be labeled a tech wonk or a finance wonk. Likewise, if you show you understand the broad range of issues faced by people in all corners of your company—and share your knowledge—you'll develop a reputation as a global thinker.

Joellyn Willis scrupulously monitored events outside her department at Square D Co., Palatine, Illinois. As a cost accountant at a plant, she absorbed considerable operational know-how. When she advanced to the internal audit staff, she used that knowledge during plant audits to help managers solve thorny problems. As a result, she says, she got requests from managers to help them with projects, even when there weren't audits. Eventually, she was named vice president of operations, a rare path for someone from the audit side.

While you're roaming around looking for ways to broaden people's perceptions of you, however, don't neglect your current assignment. "Some people are so busy looking for the next thing, they don't complete tasks," Ms. Willis says. "People who get a reputation for getting the job done will be sought out, as opposed to those who just have concepts or philosophies."

Finally, don't pigeonhole yourself by passing up opportunities for the wrong reasons. Maybe the job isn't exactly what you had in mind. Don't automatically rule it out. Ms. Willis was reluctant to leave operations for a controller's job in corporate headquarters until advised to do so by a trusted mentor. In the eye of the corporate storm, he reasoned, she would see and learn things that would benefit her later in her career. That job, she says now, was what brought her to the attention of the company's key executives.

It's up to you to realize when you've been pigeonholed, and you're the only one who's going to convince people otherwise. For starters, learn to showcase yourself in meetings.

14

CHASING THE MBA:
IS IT WORTH THE HASSLE?

The master's of business administration degree casts a powerful spell over corporate America.

The graduate degree, particularly from an elite school such as Wharton, the Tuck School of Business, Harvard, or Stanford, is probably the single most important credential a CEO wannabe could possess. Look at our big corporations; most of them are run by holders of the degree. Look at the heavy flock of major corporate entities that pour onto campuses around the country each year, wooing potential management material as if it were fraternity rush week.

Yet there is another element in the workforce that contends the degree is an unnecessary waste of time and money. Stay on the job, they say, learn as you go. Experience is the best teacher.

So who is right? The answer is as diverse as the huge population of would-be executives that fill up hundreds of MBA programs across the country every year.

Most MBA programs seek candidates who have graduated from college and had three to five years of business experience. By then, though, many people are entrenched in their career paths. Spending thousands of dollars and losing two years of career momentum is a heavy price to pay for a formal education in business management techniques.

But if learning were the only issue, this would be a no-brainer and many MBA programs would be out of business. People go to graduate business schools because the mere presence of the credential on their résumés adds considerable cachet to their careers; because the powerful alumni networks they can tap into are worth the steep price of admission; because they have plateaued or are otherwise dissatisfied with their present career momentum and this is the best way to change direction.

Are those good enough reasons to take the plunge? For many, yes.

When Ruth S. Suh started thinking about an MBA degree, some colleagues at IBM North America, where she was a sales specialist, argued that experience was more important.

But Ms. Suh has "very high" career aspirations, and it hadn't escaped her notice that most of her company's senior management held MBAs from top-ranked schools. She's also considering a career in management consulting, an MBA-intensive industry. So she decided to go for it.

"I don't necessarily think that an MBA from just any school would be to my benefit," she says. "Two years of work experience is a big sacrifice to make."

Less clear was the value of the MBA that Hoyt Gier pursued at Dartmouth's Tuck School of Business. At first, he wanted to return to the building industry he had been in for seventeen years, and even he wondered whether that industry values a degree from a prestigious school like Tuck.

That's always a consideration in these momentous decisions. Some industries don't cherish the degree as much as others; in some businesses, where technology is forcing rapid change, it is feared that someone who leaves for an MBA program will fall hopelessly behind, both in the technology and in the ever-changing political climate.

Besides, he was forty when he entered Tuck, well beyond what is considered the ideal age for business school. An employer might surmise that after seventeen years, much of that in management, an MBA had little to offer Mr. Gier.

Still, Mr. Gier must have known there was a reason for his cross-country trek into uncertainty. Two years later, he graduated a transformed person. The experience had awakened in him a hunger for Wall Street, and that's where he landed.

Marc and Brenda Mizgorski decided to interrupt their successful careers (his as a corporate controller, hers as an entrepreneur), abandon the comfortable home they were purchasing in tony Pacific Grove, California, and trek cross-country in pursuit of MBAs from the University of Pennsylvania's prestigious Wharton School. The two-year graduate program cost them an estimated $200,000 in tuition, expenses, and lost income.

Why in heaven's name would they do such a thing? The Mizgorskis were at a crossroads in their careers. Ms. Mizgorski, then thirty-one years old, says her business, providing short-term accounting services to companies, didn't feel like something she wanted to do forever. "The spark wasn't there," she says. She wanted to start an Internet-related company but felt she needed expanded managerial skills to build one of any size. The Mizgorskis also figured that attending school together would put less stress on their marriage than going consecutively over a four-year period.

Still, both understand they've taken on some risk. "We'll owe quite a bit of money when all is said and done," Mr. Mizgorski said at the time. Ms. Mizgorski added: "We have fears over everything. We both left everything."

Experts generally advise people to get into the best program that will admit them, given their grades and test scores. If you're looking to make a big splash on Wall Street or with the major consulting firms, you'd better get into one of the top twenty schools, because that's where most of them recruit. Schools that don't rate in the top twenty in the various rating services may have other attractions, such as a strong niche in a particular industry.

Mike Harrington decided to enter a joint law–MBA degree program at Gonzaga University in Spokane, Washington, reasoning that the MBA would give him an edge over other lawyers.

It worked. During interviews at Moffatt Thomas Barrett Rock & Fields in Boise, Idaho, where he became a senior associate, the MBA was much discussed, he says. "People see that having an MBA with my law degree sets me apart from your typical regional law gradu-ate," he says.

MBA programs also have local appeal, since that's where alumni generally stay, so a smaller school with a strong local alumni network would appeal to those who want to stay in a particular geographical location.

Smaller schools, especially those with part-time and executive MBA programs, also attract those who are squeezed financially or who are mainly seeking additional skills and intend to return to their original jobs. They are less attracted by alumni networks and expo-sure to big-time employers.

Mark Landregan calculates that by passing up Georgetown and instead attending the University of Missouri, Columbia, which offered a scholarship and a job as a teaching assistant, he is avoiding about $50,000 in debt. David Seaman, a development team leader with Thomson Financial Services, estimated it would take him more than ten years to recoup the cost of a top-tier program. He opted to go to Boston University.

Palmyra Pawlik credits her part-time graduate work in a technol-ogy and business graduate program at Santa Clara University for a recent promotion, even though she hasn't graduated yet. "I'm thirty years old and a manager at a leading technology company," she con-cludes. "I make in the nineties, with enough money in the bank to buy a house, the company pays for my education, and I am two pay-ments away from being totally debt-free. Why should I spend two years unpaid at a $20,000-a-year school just to mimic the experience I am already receiving?"

But beware small-school syndrome, a condition that causes company résumé screeners to toss your document onto the "miscellaneous" pile because you haven't gotten your degree from a high-ranked school.

With an MBA from Florida Atlantic University nearly in his hip pocket, David Rattner ventured out to set the corporate world ablaze.

Early on, however, he couldn't even light the match. The executive recruiters he pursued in vain don't have a problem with his work experience, he says. "What they're saying is, 'You don't have that Har-vard, Wharton pedigree. Thanks for calling.'" He then shifted his strategy to contacting companies directly.

Mr. Rattner decided to attend school part-time in his hometown of Boca Raton, Florida, so he could continue working at his father's real estate investment firm. "To leave the position I was in was ludicrous," he says. "What we were doing was far more than I could have hoped for in terms of experience."

He wanted, however, to explore opportunities in the world of big corporations.

Now he wonders: Was his decision to attend a smaller, lesser-known business school a mistake? And how can he now grab the attention of hiring managers?

Had he gone to Harvard, he says ruefully, he would have less real-world experience and more theory, but he'd be more marketable.

To catch up, graduates like Mr. Rattner from lesser-known programs must be more creative in their job search—and willing to accept some harsh realities.

For instance, there may be no alumni network to speak of; smaller schools lack the resources to build and maintain that kind of organization. So you may have to get some people together and organize one yourself.

You must also market yourself more aggressively. Each company must be approached as a separate challenge, complete with customized résumé and cover letter that shows your intimate knowledge of that company's challenges and the skills you bring to solving them.

In essence, you are your own marketing case study.

An MBA can be a real career booster, but learn first whether the school's strengths meet your specific needs, and remember: An MBA calls for making a serious investment of time and money, and in the end, only you will know if it was worth it.

15

DUNNING YOUR BOSS FOR A RAISE

Campaigning for a raise remains one of the most awkward acts of career management. Sure, you deserve it, but how do you march in and ask for one without seeming greedy and ungrateful? How do you marshal the information needed to make your case in a realm fraught with secrecy and misdirection?

Moreover, the market for raises has changed considerably over the past few years. In most cases, companies have clamped down hard on salary increases for current staff. But they've been downright profligate in paying people from other companies, particularly in areas where critical talent shortages exist.

The key, as it has always been, is gaining leverage. Those who have it get the dough. Those who don't, don't. Do you work in a hot product area, manage a major contributor to profits, or have skills the company is loath to lose? Then you've got leverage, brother.

Raises are still available for professionals and managers who "make a measurable difference to the bottom line, productivity, and customer satisfaction," says Joseph P. Clark, a project manager for an IBM subsidiary.

Mr. Clark doesn't have a hard time quantifying his worth, since he handles his unit's largest client, an easily quantifiable job. "If you can demonstrate you have run a very profitable project with high customer satisfaction and your company is moving in that direction, you've put yourself in a strong position," he says. "Those are the people who get recognized."

But what if you are an administrative manager whose job isn't easily linked to the revenue stream? Then you have to document your accomplishments. Every job offers opportunity to benefit the corporation. Perhaps something you did provided the company with a significant cost savings or increased productivity.

Keep a journal of your achievements. ("Dear Diary: Today I saved the company $2,000 by . . ." You get the idea.)

When review time rolls around, summarize the accomplishments in a memo to your boss and send it to her before the review. That will give her ammunition needed to convince higher-ups that you're worth the added dough.

Make sure you have a sense of your worth in the marketplace (see "Getting What You're Worth," page 32).

You must also work on your relationship with your boss. She's your only ally—or your biggest obstacle—in the raise wars. Make sure she's on your side when her bosses question a raise recommendation.

Your annual review is also the beginning of your next campaign for a raise. During the review, try to define what goals must be achieved in the coming year to earn a raise and how those goals will be measured.

And it helps to know your quarry. This can be difficult, because companies are notoriously secretive about their policies on raises. But you can get some clues by being observant and by pumping colleagues.

Some companies, for instance, cut down sharply on raises as employees get older. Jim Hargrove, an Austin, Texas, consultant, left corporate life when his raises stopped. "Companies think people over fifty can't find another job and pretty much have to take what they offer," he says.

How much turnover is there at your company? Some companies would rather see people walk than give in to salary demands, fearing it will start a stampede among other employees. Or they'll put ceilings on what they think a job is worth.

A corporate facilities manager, who requested anonymity, ran into that when he sought a raise. He cited his diligent research of comparable pay scales, his twenty years of experience, and his beyond-the-call-of-duty performance. The company rejected his comparisons as irrelevant in its team environment (translation: If we pay you, we'll have to pay your teammates, too) and pointedly reminded him that the job didn't really require someone with his experience.

Of course, a raise doesn't have to be in hard currency, and that could give you some wiggle room. Increasingly these days, companies are willing to offer stock options, a company car, or added time off as an alternative. Or, if they're afraid of the impact of a salary increase on their overall salary structure, they might be willing to come up with some cash in the form of a bonus that won't be reflected in your base salary.

If the company remains resistant to all your entreaties, research, and documentation, it may be time to start looking elsewhere. That's the surest way to snag a significant raise. This assumes that your skills and knowledge are in demand, of course.

Kristen Baron, a human resources specialist at Hoffmann-La Roche, the pharmaceuticals company, made two job moves that netted her $14,000 and $10,000 salary hikes in recent years. After two raises of 4 percent in four years at a Dresser Industries unit, Peter J. Rayna got a big raise—and a chance to learn new skills—by moving to a smaller company.

That weighty offer from a new employer might also rouse your old employer to action. Of course, playing the counteroffer card is dangerous. Some managers consider this an act of disloyalty (even though most of them have probably turned the trick sometime in their careers). You could get the raise and later find that your relationship with your boss has become so damaged that you're unable to perform your job. You could even be replaced at the first opportunity. Again, know your company. How have they reacted in the past when people tried to use an offer from a competitor to get a raise?

And if you decide to play this game, remember that it could be an endgame. Don't do it if you're not fully willing to leave for the new job. Because many companies will invite you to do just that, wishing you good luck as they usher you out the door with your personal possessions in a box.

Here's a case study of a successful raise campaign:

Wesley D. Millican knew, by the numerous calls he was receiving from peers and headhunters, that many jobs were available at higher pay than he was currently earning. But he liked his job as vice president of physician services for Physician Reliance Network, which manages medical practices. So instead of entertaining offers, he decided to ask for a raise.

Mr. Millican plotted his campaign carefully. Not wanting to catch his boss by surprise, he requested a meeting, at the boss's convenience, to discuss his compensation package. "People need time to research what the market is," he says about giving his boss notice.

He wrote a proposal, including his research on pay for comparable positions, the money he wanted, and why he thought he deserved a raise. It allowed him to marshal his arguments and edit his thoughts before the meeting. Also, the memo provided his boss with something concrete to present to other executives involved in the decision.

In the memo, Mr. Millican made it clear he wasn't shopping around and stressed how much he wanted to stay with the company. That allowed him to mention offers that were coming to him without making it look as if he were delivering an ultimatum. In raise negotiations, too many people adopt an "if I don't get this, I'll leave" approach, he says. "Your intention shouldn't be to make demands, but to make sure your compensation is up to market standards."

In the memo, Mr. Millican also provided detailed facts and figures about how he contributed to the company's success, a must when seeking a raise. "I could show that I was more productive than comparable people in other organizations," he says, basing the comparisons on his past experience and on current information about staffing in the industry.

In this cost-conscious, performance-driven economy, your financial needs are irrelevant to raise discussions. The best argument is that you are below market value for your position and you couldn't be easily replaced, because of your expertise, the tight job market, or some combination of those factors.

Some final tips: Every company has its cultural idiosyncrasies, so interview veteran managers to learn how your company handles raise requests.

Present specific salary targets; if you offer a range, your boss will generally choose the lower end of the range.

Know when to stop negotiating. If the boss won't budge on salary, try for a bonus, stock options, or added responsibility. "Money may come with added responsibility," Mr. Millican says, "but even if it doesn't, you've got something you can market to someone else for more money."

Whatever you do, don't end the talks on a sour note. Mr. Millican got a substantial raise, although not as much as he had requested. He decided it was more important that both sides walk away happy. Creating a good work environment after negotiations, he says, is "more important to your career in the long run."

When asking for a raise, plot your campaign beforehand: know you're worth more by studying the market, and show you're worth more by detailing your accomplishments.

PART THREE

Into the Management Maelstrom

16

AVOIDING THOSE FIRST-TIME
MANAGER BLUES

There you are, footloose and fancy-free, a successful role player in your organizational hierarchy. You're making pretty good money, and you actually know what you're doing! After all, it's what you trained and studied for all those years.

Then suddenly there's a phone call, and in the time it takes you to get to your boss's office, it's all over.

You're now a manager, and may the good Lord protect you. Now, it no longer matters how good you are at your job or how much you know; your future hinges on your ability to organize and put a charge into a group of malcontents, slackers, and Machiavellian schemers. Plus, you've now got a bunch of higher-ups perched on your shoulder, just waiting for you to screw up.

Okay, making the leap to management isn't quite that traumatic, but it's close. Most get thrown into the arena undertrained and underarmed, uncertain how much authority they really have and just how to wield it without alienating this gaggle of needy humans they've been asked to lead. Sure, companies talk a lot about training, mentoring, and management support. They assure their fledgling bosses that they are patient and tolerant of mistakes. But that's not the picture many new managers see. "After a promotion," says Sari Factor, a vice president at a textbook publisher, "there's an automatic expectation that you know what to do."

No wonder the failure rate for first-time managers is so high (an estimated 40 percent). And if you go into this new career phase thinking primarily about the perks and privileges you'll enjoy, you'll likely become another statistic. But this shaky bridge can be crossed by morphing yourself into a different kind of corporate creature who thinks more broadly about the task at hand.

New managers can easily get disoriented. After all, everything they've known is now largely nonessential. When Jack Adams first became a manager at the old Bell Laboratories, it took him a while to realize that "being a technical wizard was not what management had in mind for me when they considered me for promotion."

In fact, as most managers learn, he had to put aside such childish things. He wasn't going to get rewarded for his technical knowledge; he would be judged on his ability to mesh a group of ten engineers into an effective team. Having been part of that team complicated matters. "These were the same folks you sat down and had lunch with and made fun of the boss with," he says. "Now they knew and you knew that you would be the subject of those comments."

Most new managers struggle with the question of how close they can get to their old pals now that they're the boss. In truth, the relationship can never be the same, because these are now people you must evaluate honestly and sometimes even dismiss. That doesn't mean you should totally distance yourself. After all, it was probably your ability to relate with people that got you the job in the first place. Turning aloof and distant doesn't win hearts and loyalty. Mr. Adams, who eventually reverted to the expert role after years as a manager, says that self-deprecating humor was his salvation. "When the group realized that I hadn't had a frontal lobotomy and turned into a 'management type,' good interpersonal relations resumed," he says.

Another typical new manager gaffe: focusing primarily on your staff and its performance. You're in the big leagues now, and you must turn in your microscope for a panoramic camera. You are now in the middle of the corporate tornado. You must manage the perceptions of your bosses and managers in other departments. Your success could depend on their support and goodwill. Will you be able to get the staff and budget you need from your boss? Will you get the co-operation needed from other departments to complete your projects successfully?

To accomplish this, 3M executive David Le Cheminant studies the priorities and needs of other departments. When he had to make budget pitches in his early managerial days at Megahertz Corp., Mr. Le Cheminant went into the meetings armed with that kind of infor-mation. "I could weave into the talk what other operations in the company had to do for my project to work," he recalls. Others didn't; "they would think their little bailiwick was the center of the corpo-rate universe," he says.

So how do you develop your own managerial style? Companies, with some exceptions, rarely provide sufficient managerial training. And it's often tough to get superiors to serve as role models. "Bosses promote people to get help with big workloads, so they tend not to want to spend time coaching," Ms. Factor says. "And new managers think if they ask too many questions, they won't look very compe-tent." She suggests getting help from other managers and from con-tacts outside the company, such as in professional groups.

But your bosses could provide some mentoring, even if they don't want to. Here's a good exercise for any new manager: Sit down with a notebook and analyze both good and bad past bosses. What did they do well that you'd like to emulate? What did they do poorly that you want to avoid? Mr. Le Cheminant learned a critical lesson from a for-mer boss's shortcomings. "She knew the business, but she didn't know how to manage creative people," he says. Her tendency to microman-age was the kiss of death to maverick creative types. "You have to understand that your job is to monitor their progress, but not to interfere with their job. You have to realize there are ten ways to skin a cat and your way is no longer the right way."

Time out here for a personal rant. I've seen "my way or the high-way" managers succeed—for a time. Usually, though, that style wears mighty threadbare (see "Chainsaw" Al Dunlop, wherever he is). And in my view, those managers fall short in the most critical way: they don't develop their people. Control-freak managers create robots who can't function unless fearless leader is giving marching orders. Successful managers get results; they also develop independent thinkers who become the next wave of successful managers.

Your first and most important task as a new manager is to understand the corporate structure and culture. Without that understanding, managing well will be exceedingly difficult, if not impossible.

17

WHO SAID TECHIES CAN'T MANAGE?

The stereotype is near indelible. Techies are shy, inward types whose idea of socializing is a saucy discussion of algorithms. Put them in polite company and they shrink against the wall. Ask them to manage? They'd be as out of place as Stone Cold Steve Austin at a royal tea party.

Which is why some companies have created separate career tracks for the technologically gifted, allowing them to advance their careers without suffering the indignity of failure as a manager. But where is it written that the technologically oriented can't learn to manage? Truth be told, many companies stall the careers of talented techies because they can't afford to let them walk away from their computers. A top-notch Java programmer is harder to replace than a general manager.

But why should techies be spared the miseries—I mean, joys—of management, with its demanding superiors, conniving peers, and mewling subordinates? With a little spit and polish, they, too, can command and motivate in the time-honored fashion.

Alan Page did it.

As far back as he can remember, Mr. Page was a card-carrying techie, interested in all things electric and electronic. As a child, he preferred plugging in the Christmas tree to opening presents. He took a course in FORTRAN programming in the seventh grade.

In his first job, he fixed computer systems. In his second, he designed databases for a consumer research company. Then, in June 1995, he joined Mott's Inc., a Stamford, Connecticut, food company, as a database analyst.

He had hoped his new job would take him beyond technological fix-up projects and into the realm of using technology to advance the business. In time, it did—but it wasn't easy. As usual, forces were conspiring to keep him in his subordinate place. To bust out, he had to learn those parts of the business that extended beyond his desk, navigate tricky office politics, and figure out how to influence nontechnical people who were sometimes suspicious and territorial. Most of all, he had to transform his image from that of a support person to that of a strategic thinker.

Initially assigned to marketing, Mr. Page found himself at odds from the start with the information technology department. Whenever he wanted to access a database, he was told to request the data he needed and IT would fetch it for him. By default, he also became the technological fix-it person, inundated with projects from befuddled managers that kept him too tied up to promote himself or his ideas. "I would drift back to fixing things, because I was comfortable with that," he says. "I thought, If I fix this, that person will be happy."

Mr. Page turned in frustration to executive coach Laura Berman Fortgang, who tried to teach him how to say no to pleading superiors and avoid becoming a dumping ground for everyone's tech problems. Once dug out from under the pile, he could start promoting his ideas. She had him put proposals on paper, stressing how the ideas would affect the company's bottom line. It was an important skill. "I'd been to engineering school, not business school, and now I'm in marketing with . . . MBAs," he says.

He sold Mott's management on a limited Internet experiment, aimed mostly at promoting awareness of Mott's products with recipes and kids' games. But those pesky senior managers kept asking about the ROI (return on investment). "I couldn't prove that we would sell more apple juice on the Web," he says.

So he honed his business skills by attending marketing presentations. He learned how marketers made assumptions to project sales. He studied the graphs and charts speakers handed out. He started practicing his presentations with Ms. Fortgang and with his wife, who would tell him where he should replace technical details with simplified, real-world analogies. "It took me a while," he says. "I had to work with marketing people to learn how to structure my answers for management."

The meetings also gave him a platform to promote his ideas. But he still had to learn how to communicate with these alien marketing beings. At first, Mr. Page had the typical techie's certainty that his way was the way of the future. "There were definitely meetings where I'd say, 'This is how it is and what we should do,'" he says. "That ruffled some feathers."

He soon adopted a gentler approach, seeking the views of others on his proposals and studying colleagues at meetings to learn what they wanted to accomplish and how his projects affected them. "That's something, as a pure tech person, I hadn't thought about," he says. Before going to meetings, he imagined possible compromises, asking himself, Is there a lesser win I can be happy with?

He attempted to mute opposition by embracing their position. "I'd try to get it out on the table right away by saying, 'I know you guys want to do this, so let's start there and work back.'"

Mr. Page strongly recommends that techies find a mentor from a different department who has a broad view of the company's issues and a pool of contacts throughout the company. It was partly his inability to find a mentor that drove him to an outside coach. Ms. Fortgang provided "just-in-time training" for him. "As issues came up, I could bounce them off her," he says.

He has risen from database analyst to manager of business intelligence systems. While he hasn't landed in a VP's chair yet, Mr. Page believes he has changed colleagues' perceptions of him. He was seen as someone who could fix tech problems but not business problems. Now, he says, "I'm the guy who can show people how to use the Web." Product managers are besieging him with questions about Web-based marketing and inviting him to their department meetings.

To break free of the techie shackles and claim your managerial birthright, you've got to demonstrate a knowledge of the business beyond your own narrow niche.

18

MANAGING TECHIES WHEN
YOU AREN'T ONE

Among the most sacred of the sacred scrolls passed down by the new age career management gurus is the one proclaiming the absolute necessity of immersing yourself in technology in order to survive in the new economy.

What a shocker. Technology is, undeniably, the wave of the future, and the more of it you absorb the better. But to succeed in the new millennium, must you spout technical jargon and be proficient at translating documents written in symbolic computer languages that make ancient Cyrillic texts read like the Berenstain Bears by comparison?

Of course not. Consider Paul Schaffer, a political science major who once envisioned a future analyzing Southeast Asian policy issues. Instead, he now manages a Sun Microsystems group that fixes bugs (the computer software variety) for distraught customers. And while he knows his way around a computer pretty well for a poly sci major, he doesn't do any of the real techie stuff, like writing software code. During meetings, he often jots down technical jargon so he can look up the meaning later.

So how did he come to reign over a cadre of code-writing, jargon-spouting engineers? As a University of Massachusetts, Amherst, undergraduate seeking a summer internship in Washington, D.C., he interviewed with the usual Beltway suspects—congressional staff, think tanks, and so on. But he also talked to Digital Equipment Corp., which offered him an internship researching the amount of money used in foreign aid grants for technical upgrades. "What sold it for me," he recalls, "was when they told me that I'd have my own office and I'd never have to make copies for anyone but myself. I thought, Wow, this is real work."

Mr. Schaffer certainly wasn't intimidated by the prospect of working in a high-tech business with a low-tech background. After all, he had the ultimate role model. His father, William Schaffer, a Sun Microsystems manager, had literally written the book on the subject (*High-Tech Careers for Lo-Tech People*).

So Mr. Schaffer began the process he calls "building context" in his career. The research experience at Digital was the context that got him his next job, with a database mapping company. As an aerial photography programs specialist, he arranged for all the aerial photography, digitized the shots, and fed them into the database. That built even more context for his next job, at a computer game maker, where he acquired and digitized images from the British Open for a computer golf game.

Meanwhile, he tracked potential jobs in technology-oriented settings that didn't involve engineering or writing code. And it dawned on him that they constituted the majority of the technology pie. "Engineering is a big part of what these companies do, but a bigger part is 'other,'" he says. "Other" includes program management, quality assurance, marketing, packaging, support, and finance.

The ability he exhibited to launch and manage a project got him a job at Sun, creating the initial consumer testing of new products, known as beta testing. "They were looking for someone who could take a program from nothing and build it," he explains.

To this point, though, he had managed to skirt around the periphery of hard-core technology. Then, he walked into his boss's office one day just as the boss was drawing up a job description for a manager who would oversee the solving of technical complaints from customers. That meant heading up a team of engineers to track down and fix glitches buried deep in the impenetrable coding language of software programs. Could anything be more technical?

But Mr. Schaffer saw it as managing relationships—in this case between the customer and the engineers—and convinced his boss he was the man for the job. "Someone has to manage that complaint, hold the customer's hand, draw up an action plan, and follow up to make sure people are doing the right things," he says. That didn't require technical know-how.

The central realization here is that most of the skills needed to be a successful manager in a high-tech company—in any company, for that matter—have little to do with technical expertise. You need to study up on your product, what it does, and how customers use it, yes; you don't want to end up as *Dilbert* fodder. But you don't have to make it or fix it yourself. A nontechnical manager can succeed, as long as he's wise enough to know what he doesn't know and recruits a strong, loyal, technical aide-de-camp. Likewise, a technically knowledgeable manager often needs a good program manager to take care of the messy details. "It's hard to find someone who can do it all," Mr. Schaffer says.

In fact, nontechies often have advantages in technical management positions, because they're not inclined to take on too much. Mr. Schaffer tells of one manager who continues to spend time working on bug fixes. "There's something wrong there," he says. "You have to have a lot of time for people as a manager."

And nontechies enter the game with fewer preconceived notions, often an advantage. That means they're frequently more receptive to new ideas or people. Mr. Schaffer talks about one successful new hire who lacked experience in writing code. He hired the man in spite of that because he "knew how the interaction between customer and engineer was supposed to work." Meanwhile, a fellow Sun manager kept an engineering job open for a year because he couldn't find someone with the right combination of skills. But what good does an empty desk do you? In that time, Mr. Schaffer contends, he could have hired someone and taught him or her the requisite skills. "Everyone wants all-stars," he says. "I want smart people who work well together."

As a nontechnical manager surrounded by tech whizzes, Mr. Schaffer does a lot of listening and has learned to trust his staff's judgment. "They know their jobs better than you do," he says. "They'll make stuff happen if you tell them where you want to go. But if you tell them how to get there, they won't have the flexibility they need and you'll probably be wrong."

But when called upon to make a managerial decision, he doesn't hesitate. That's where many trip up. "You learn the process of controlled failure," he says. "If you make ten decisions, you know two of them will be wrong. I'm not afraid to fail. Nothing is ever so broke it can't be fixed. Some managers can't make decisions because they're afraid to make wrong decisions."

In his own career decisions, Mr. Schaffer looks for positions that will add something to his skills and thus lead him to the next step. His current job, for example, requires him to set up and manage remote locations around the world, a valuable add-on experience in an increasingly global business environment.

"Technology changes," he concludes. "Engineers today will be obsolete ten years from now, but management, leadership, building processes—they haven't changed in a thousand years."

You don't need a degree in electrical engineering to manage a tech staff, but you do need to build a close relationship with your staff by listening carefully and knowing what it is you don't know.

19

MANAGING A HOSTILE CREW

Sooner or later, it will happen: You will be asked to manage a staff of people who, for some reason, consider you the Antichrist before they've even met you. Maybe they're still mourning the departure of a beloved boss, or you're coming from a different department and they resent it. Or maybe they're just a headstrong, ornery crew with a healthy dislike for authority. Why did you think the job was open?

In 1995, Carl Friedrich was asked to manage a crab pot of cantankerous physicians for New York's Hospital for Special Surgery. You must grasp the degree of difficulty here: doctors are a lone-wolf breed accustomed to playing God, and they don't take orders well. In this case, Mr. Friedrich laments, each of the doctors did things differently and were as resistant to change as a hardy new bacterial strain. "It was like trying to merge twenty little businesses at once," he says.

Moreover, Mr. Friedrich started with three strikes against him: he was an outsider, a nonphysician, and a soon-to-be MBA holder—all blood-red flags for set-in-their-ways hospital veterans.

Now there's a real test of your managerial skills. What do you do? Here's what Mr. Friedrich did, and while the health care business may be idiosyncratic, the leadership lessons he learned are universal.

First, he assessed his staff's perception of him. "There was a lot of myth about what my intentions were," he says. "I was thought to be a cost cutter, someone who would tell them no."

In fact, while he didn't consider himself a hatchet man, Mr. Friedrich did have ambitious plans to improve operations. Based on this assessment, though, he wisely backed away from his staff initially. He had to win their trust and confidence before he could hope to sell them on major, life-changing programs. "The biggest mistake someone in my role can make is trying to produce the master plan," he says. "You're asking too much of people to try to change that quickly."

He instead opted for less controversial efforts sure to show a quick return. It wasn't difficult, for example, to convince the doctors to combine supplies purchasing to earn bigger discounts. That was something everyone understood, and the subsequent profit gains earned him some brownie points.

So he trotted out a proposal to consolidate their billing operations, which he considered a surefire and noncontroversial money saver. But when it came to their precious financial records, the doctors dug in their heels, smelling a managed care cost-cutting effort. Plus, they were reluctant to share information with each other. "I was getting into shouting matches with physicians about things that other businessmen would laugh about," Mr. Friedrich says.

Rather than forcing the issue, Mr. Friedrich formed a billing consortium and then lobbied the doctors, one by one, to join. He spent a year cajoling one stubborn clinician. She finally acceded and found that more accurate and efficient billing boosted her revenues by 40 percent and shrank her costs 30 percent. Naturally, she became a big fan of the system, and soon others started joining.

Mr. Friedrich also sought to assure his physicians that he wasn't some arrogant, MBA ideologue trying to turn them into medical mechanics who no longer had decision-making authority. "I told them I wouldn't force anything on them that compromised them as physicians," he says.

Where some managers would have simply chosen the lowest-cost suppliers, Mr. Friedrich offered them options to make them feel they still had clout in the operation. "You try to give them options, but limit the options," he says.

He allowed two medical groups with different billing software to keep their own systems, as long as they met minimum performance standards he set. When one group's software couldn't meet the standards, 90 percent of them switched.

The most important management skill he learned, however, was shutting up and listening. By doing so, he discovered that most of his doctors' complaints weren't really directed at him. "They just want to tell it to someone," he says. "They want someone to be their advocate."

Consider the physician who complained about a shabby sign that he felt was conveying a negative image of the hospital. With all that was going on, a run-down sign seemed a low-priority item to Mr. Friedrich. When it hadn't been replaced a month later, however, the physician exploded at a staff meeting. "The issue seemed trivial to me, but it was critical to him," Mr. Friedrich says.

It wasn't so much the importance of the issue as the physician's feeling that his concerns weren't considered important. Spending the few minutes necessary to order a new sign would have prevented an ugly incident.

By not taking care of the little things, he wasn't winning the trust he needed to accomplish the big things. "If they think you don't care, they won't listen to the bold plan you have," he says.

And no matter how compelling those plans are and how brilliant you are as a manager, it will all come to naught if the staff stays hostile.

To manage a hostile crew, you must defuse the hostility. The best way to do that is to understand its roots and take actions that clearly show the hostility is unwarranted.

20

THE ART AND CRAFT OF BEING
A GOOD NUMBER TWO

Here's to the loyal second banana, who sweats the details while numero uno collects the accolades.

It isn't easy to be a good number two in corporate America. You must bolster your leader's ego while checking yours at the door. You must seek credit without upstaging the boss. At times, you must find ways to object without being objectionable.

Yet business schools and corporations, with their never-ending obsession with leadership, fail miserably in teaching people how to fill the crucial role of top lieutenant.

The first responsibility of a good number two is to win the boss's trust. And that takes time, says Amanda Rose, who filled that role as executive director of Stanford Coaching, a privately held New York company that tutors students for college entrance exams.

Ms. Rose built that trust by "knowing what I can and can't reveal" to others, by knowing that when the news media calls, her boss speaks for the company, and by showing a united front to the staff.

That doesn't mean being a yes-person. Ms. Rose recalls a staff meeting where she and her boss clearly had different opinions. "I stated my opinion, then Lisa said, 'That's Amanda's opinion, here are my thoughts,'" she says. Most times, she adds, compromises can be worked out.

And if they can't? Another part of being a good subordinate is remembering who's boss. "I will probably capitulate," Ms. Rose says. You can't be a good number two with an "I'll show you" attitude, she explains.

Mostly, a good subordinate executes. "I don't need someone who's going to give me huge ideas or create the map from the ground up," says Lisa Jacobson, Stanford Coaching's president. "I need someone who's going to make the map detailed and implement it."

She also wants someone who is direct and clear, with an open-minded attitude and a can-do spirit. "I want someone who says, 'It's going to be okay, this is under control,'" she says.

Perpetual agreement isn't required, but the aide must pick her battles. "You can't do it all the time," Ms. Jacobson says.

If your ambition is to eventually be a number one, you must find ways to shine in this supportive role. As Wee Willie Keeler, the old baseballer, once said about successful hitting: "Hit 'em where they ain't." In this case, find areas of responsibility that the boss doesn't covet or doesn't have time for. "There are so many things to do that the sheriff couldn't always be there," says Michael Emerson of his stint as a deputy at a big advertising agency. "That's your time to shine."

Sometimes you shine by handling the minutiae of the business plan or by demonstrating interest and enthusiasm during meetings, Mr. Emerson says. He says he listens carefully at meetings, picking issues for himself that complement what the boss stresses while demonstrating his own expertise.

Whatever you do, the boss expects you to do it without bothering her. "My challenge is to assume that responsibility without going to her and saying, 'What do I do? I never did this before,'" Ms. Rose says.

Being a loyal deputy can get tricky if your boss's interest and that of the company diverge. Going against your boss could damage your career. But if the company is damaged, everyone's career will suffer. It's a tough spot to be in. My advice? Make your case to the boss first. Make it respectfully but forcefully, stressing that you feel the situation could damage him as a leader and you want to prevent that. If he still pursues this course, you have a decision to make: How serious a situation is it? It had better be darned critical to the company before you take it to the board or go public with it. You might even consider finding a new job to distance yourself from it.

Loyalty, tempered by honesty and a willingness to sweat the details, are the hallmarks of the best number twos.

PART FOUR

MAKING MIDCOURSE CORRECTIONS

21

TURNAROUNDS AND CAREERS:
EVEN A LEMON HAS JUICE

I once faced a crucial decision in my career. Should I accept an offered manager's position in a department that was in a shambles? Or should I wait for an expected opening in a department that ran like a well-oiled machine?

I sought advice from a sage former boss. His answer was brief and simple: If I opted for the presumably safer job, I had nowhere to go but down. Even if I were able to maintain the department's high performance level, would I get credit for it? About the best review I could hope for was "Well, at least he didn't screw it up."

Ask Gene Bartow, Larry Brown, Gary Cunningham, Larry Farmer, Jim Harrick, and Steve Lavin. All have been winning basketball coaches at UCLA. Unfortunately, they all followed John Wooden, the icon of college basketball coaches and winner of ten national championships. Not surprisingly, all were found wanting by fickle fans and boosters.

The lesson is clear: If you want to make a name for yourself as a can-do manager, find something broken that needs to be fixed. Patti Lewis held high-profile management positions at Procter & Gamble, Mattel, Tyco, and Tonka. She got needed advertising experience at none other than J. Walter Thompson. She could have parlayed that into a prime position at almost any consumer products company.

Instead, she went up to Harlem to fix a broken doll.

Doll collectors have always cherished the high-priced, handcrafted Madame Alexander dolls, but they were supposedly relics in an age of mass markets, automation, and low-cost Asian knockoffs. So why did she accept a position as senior vice president of marketing for the Harlem-based company in 1994? For one thing, the chance to resuscitate a storied, seventy-two-year-old company seemed exciting.

Of course, you have to be reasonable about it. Some companies just can't be rescued. Ms. Lewis studied the company for four months, besieging officers and others in the industry with challenging questions. Was there a market for the product? Was there customer loyalty she could build on? How much of a threat was the competition? Were the company's major shareholders in for the long haul? How much were they willing to invest in growth? How stable was the workforce after a period of hard times?

She came up with a lot of positive answers. The collectibles market at that time was being stimulated by the entry of Mattel's Barbie Collectibles, and Alexander enjoyed loyal customers and a solid reputation. Competition was "real, but manageable," she recalls, and sufficient funding existed to support a turnaround plan.

But, as she learned, you'd better have a strong stomach for this kind of work, because there are always surprises, most of them unpleasant. A week after she joined the company, she learned it needed additional financing to continue operations, and management wanted her to spearhead the search, a role for which she had no previous experience. A reason to bail out? Not to Ms. Lewis, who saw it instead as a chance to learn important new skills. She immersed herself in finance and manufacturing in order to woo investors, dealt with the press, and even learned about bankruptcy proceedings (the company filed for court protection that year).

It was downright scary. Vendors stopped shipping and employees froze over crucial decisions. When a trade publication reported the company's imminent demise, investors and interested buyers flooded Ms. Lewis with faxes.

But when new investors bought the company at a bankruptcy court auction, it was Ms. Lewis they sought to run it. Within ninety days, with the help of a new, streamlined manufacturing process borrowed from the Japanese and a cash infusion, she returned the company to profitability.

All well and good, you say, but what does it take to succeed at this tension-laden art of financial brinkmanship?

Here's the profile. Do you fit?

The turnaround manager must always stay calm and think clearly in the midst of turmoil and be able to envision both short- and long-term goals. She must be able to pull together an emergency business plan and get it into operation at flank speed. She needs to know more about finance than the average manager, since that's a critical part of any decision in a turnaround. She must be extremely persuasive and able to inspire confidence in order to cope with the almost constant conflict and tension.

When Al Koch took over in 1997 as interim finance chief for Oxford Health Plans, a troubled managed care company, he had to quickly raise millions of dollars, fend off antsy regulators in five states, slash budgets, reassure physicians and hospitals that hadn't been paid, and prepare for an onslaught of regulatory audits and consumer lawsuits. And he had to do all that before the company's creditors lost patience and closed shop.

In the midst of that turmoil, an aide pointed out an error in the turnaround plan that could have significant consequences. Mr. Koch calmly brainstormed with the man, and a correction was made. "Man, nothing bothers you," Mr. Koch recalls the manager saying. The lesson: "It's important to act in a way that won't panic people who are already close to panic," says Mr. Koch, a managing principal with Jay Alix & Associates, a turnaround management firm that has been called in to rescue everything from a topless bar to Service Merchandise, the big Brentwood, Tennessee, retailer.

"I liken our business to ambulance driving," he says. "When we arrive at the scene of an accident, there are bodies everywhere. We focus more on saving the bodies than on figuring out how the accident happened."

Sage advice. To be successful, a turnaround manager has to get people's eyes off the wreckage and focused on the road ahead—and has to do it quickly. That means he or she must pull together a recovery plan quickly and sell it to dispirited, and often hostile, shareholders, creditors, and suppliers. All have different agendas, and emotions can boil over. Mr. Koch says some of his colleagues have received death threats from people fearing the loss of jobs or big investments.

To win over the skeptics and build confidence, focus on small, achievable victories first. The big stuff can come later. You'll need a strong constitution, because there is always pain in a turnaround: cutbacks that have to made, people who have to be let go. And whatever you do, you must do it quickly. "There's a point at which you have enough information to act," Ms. Lewis says. "If you wait to get everything, you're too late."

It's tough on the old nervous system, but remember: If you pull it off, companies and recruiters will start beating a path to your door.

Turning around a sick operation, whether a department or an entire organization, isn't easy. It requires fast thinking, nerves of steel, and the ability to refocus people's attention. But a turnaround will do more for your long-term career than taking over a well-oiled machine.

22

SOMEONE WILL BENEFIT
FROM A COMPANY CRISIS;
WHY SHOULDN'T IT BE YOU?

You've just found out that your company is in deep doo-doo. What's your first instinct? Update your résumé? Drain a six-pack? Run for the hills?

Here's another thought: Stick around and look for the opportunities.

First of all, what have you got to lose? The damage has been done; bailing out now won't make you look any better to future employers. Ah, but if you stay and the company is resurrected, you're an instant star. Name me one company that wouldn't trip all over itself trying to recruit someone known for resuscitating the corporate dead.

Moreover, the crisis will thin out the competition. Some will pack up and go; others will get the ax. Lines of authority will become blurred, and there will be ample opportunity to step outside your current responsibilities and earn a reputation as a take-charge manager.

When Sykes Datatronics, a Rochester, New York, telecommunications supplier, lurched to the edge of bankruptcy in the 1980s, Randi Winterman had just joined the company as manager of technical communications. Did she bemoan her rotten deal? Hardly. The crisis allowed her to take over all communications functions. She also volunteered for the management team evaluating the company's properties.

"It allowed me, as a thirty-year-old person, to gain insight into what's involved in running a company, to gain access to people a young middle manager would never have access to," she says. Ms. Winterman says the experience gave her the confidence to start her own consulting firm and advise companies on strategic planning issues.

Just months after Jill McCurdy joined Koss Corp. in 1984 as a trainer of salespeople, the consumer electronics company filed for bankruptcy court protection, axed half of its staff, and asked the survivors to absorb the work left behind by the dear departed. Lenore Lillie jumped on the sinking ship three months after the bankruptcy filing as a temp in purchasing.

"You could smell the opportunity," Ms. McCurdy says.

Yes indeed. Ms. McCurdy is now vice president of product development; Ms. Lillie has risen to vice president of operations. Both say the company's hard times generated career opportunities they might never have gotten otherwise.

"We were in such desperate straits, we didn't rely on conventional ways of doing things," says CEO Michael Koss. "They might have been passed over before for someone with more experience."

Ms. Lillie started as little more than a gofer. But with only one other person left in the purchasing department, she soon found herself sorting out suppliers who were willing to give the company some financial leeway and finding replacements for those who wouldn't. She also displayed an eagerness to take on more than one job, which caught the eye of the beleaguered marketing manager, who "saw me as someone he could teach things to," Ms. Lillie says.

Others noticed her initiative as well. Soon she was installing a new system for reporting supply shortages and dispersing data from the company's mainframe to PCs to make sales analysis less cumbersome. She spent a year in public relations, then was named an administrative sales manager. The company heaped domestic purchasing and inventory control on her plate and, eventually, Asian purchasing.

Talk about your instant MBA!

Ms. McCurdy was seeking a less bureaucratic environment when she left a big, heavy-equipment maker and joined Koss. She got more than she bargained for. "It was like being thrown off the pier," she says.

But, she adds, troubled Koss listened to younger people. It didn't have much choice. "I thought this would be an environment I would do well in," she says.

Like Ms. Lillie, she waded through multiple assignments (at one point, she was even Ms. Lillie's boss). "The more I got to do, the more excited I got," she says.

In 1994, the company combined engineering and marketing into product development—something akin to merging the Hatfields and the McCoys—and put Ms. McCurdy in charge. "It was a gutsy move to combine them and an even gutsier one putting me in charge," she marvels.

Ms. McCurdy credits her unlikely rise to Michael Koss's ability to spot potential and the company's financial difficulties. "The bankruptcy filing got rid of a lot of competition and made the path a lot clearer," she says.

Of course, it takes the right person to charge down that path, which isn't always an easy one. Someone willing to take on jobs where the responsibility exceeds his knowledge, but who learns quickly enough to catch up. Someone with great energy and concentration, because he will be juggling many balls through long hours. Someone self-confident and polished enough to offer honest, and sometimes opposing, opinions to senior management in a way that doesn't offend. Someone willing to make tough decisions quickly and live with the consequences, a prerequisite in any turnaround situation.

The ride can be harrowing, but for those willing to chance it, the rewards are enormous.

A *company in crisis is like a buffet table full of opportunity for managers willing to belly up to the table.*

23

LEARNING FROM FAILURE:
OVERCOMING HUBRIS

Above all things, young hotshot execs especially, beware hubris.

It is the curse of this modern age, this feeling of "I'm going to change the world" invincibility. And it has led to the downfall of many a good career.

For an object lesson in this deadly sin, look no further than Umang Gupta. In the 1980s, he turned his vision of software to manage databases for vast personal computer networks into a hot Silicon Valley company that bore his name. Gupta Corporation's value peaked at $400 million—a pretty ripe number in those days—and Mr. Gupta's personal wealth hit nearly $100 million "for a few days," he says.

But powerful new competitors sent the company into a tailspin— seven straight unprofitable quarters and a plummeting stock price. In 1996, Mr. Gupta quit as CEO and the company changed its name to Centura Software.

He says he ignored storm warnings of market change, partly because he listened only to his own voice. That voice was chanting a familiar Silicon Valley mantra: "The company wasn't a company, it was a cause," he says. "We were going to . . ." You know the rest.

That attitude drives many of today's high-tech entrepreneurs, but it's a double-edged sword. While it motivates idealistic young techno-wizards to great heights, it also blinds them to market realities. For every super-rich new technology tycoon, there's a broken heart who overestimated the value of his technology or underestimated the resources needed to capture the market.

Mr. Gupta is trying to adapt the lessons he learned from his set-back to his current role as chairman and CEO of Keynote Systems. Having completed a successful public offering last year, the company has now entered the hubris danger zone.

You wouldn't have pegged Mr. Gupta as a hubris victim when he started Gupta Corporation. This wasn't some wild and woolly young techie with a program. He was an experienced businessman, an MBA holder, a veteran of IBM and Oracle. At Oracle, he was the seven-teenth employee and helped pen the business plan.

But he had always dreamed of being an entrepreneur, and that's a powerful narcotic. He launched Gupta on a shoestring, bypassing venture capitalists and financing growth with fees from early cus-tomers, such as Lotus and Computer Associates, which bought into his concept.

It's a risky strategy, leaving you with little financial cushion if well-heeled competitors home in on your market. Still, the company grew to $56 million in annual revenues by the time it went public in 1993.

The euphoria didn't last long; Microsoft and Oracle, among oth-ers, piled into the market, and Gupta's performance tumbled. Oracle offered to buy the company, but Mr. Gupta declined. This was a mis-sion; how could he sell it? It's a decision he now regrets.

Mr. Gupta sank into a period of dark reflection. Why didn't he see the market shift coming? "I started to think of all the things I should have done to make the company outlast me," he says.

In today's Silicon Valley, unfortunately, this problem is all too com-mon. Too many companies are forged around the vision of a single founder. They're doomed to falter unless the founder surrounds him-self with a savvy team and heeds their advice, particularly as the com-pany outgrows his initial vision. "No individual is smart enough to figure out all the technological moves," Mr. Gupta says. "Bill Gates and Larry Ellison have done it, but they also built organizations that can react to change."

Mr. Gupta's single-mindedness also caused him to miss the importance of the Internet. "I had people leaving Gupta to go to a little company named Netscape in 1994," he says. "Why didn't I pay attention?"

After he left Gupta in 1995, the downcast executive traveled and read a book a day. He joined the board of Keynote, which measures the performance of commercial websites, but vowed to stay away from a leadership role. The lure of running a company again was too strong, however, and when the board asked him to take over as CEO, he accepted.

This time, he vows, things will be different. For one thing, he figures the company is less likely to fall victim to hubris because it is built around a variety of technological services instead of a single technological revolution.

But unless Mr. Gupta surrounds himself with the best and the brightest and puts them in a position to make quick decisions based on their market analyses, history will repeat itself.

He says he has. "You don't hire people to do what you say," he advises. "You hire people to worry for you." The less he worries about what they're doing, he says, the better he judges their performance to be.

He also must make time for his staff, to ensure that he hears the unvarnished truth. This, too, he vows to do, carving swatches of time out of his usually frenetic pace of meetings to brainstorm with staff. He also leaves more time to take the pulse of the industry at conferences and seminars.

If he follows through, the company has a fighting chance for success, even if powerful competitors again attack him or new business trends swing the industry in a different direction.

Solicit opinions, then make your decisions, but don't listen only to yourself. Remember: Pride goeth before a fall.

24

ADAPTING TO CONTINUAL TURMOIL

Kathy Reed is a study in adaptability. In her career, she has survived management shake-ups, reorganizations, strategic about-faces, and reductions in workforce. And she did it, for the most part, by calculating where the greatest corporate itch was and then getting in position to scratch it.

For more than twenty years, she kept her corporate career alive and advancing this way. Eventually those winds blew her away from corporate life and into her own business, again just before such moves became fashionable.

Ms. Reed is a corporate chameleon, constantly adapting to change and putting herself in the right place to benefit. "It's everyone's job to stay up on what's going on and what the company needs," she says.

From the start, she was a different kind of animal. After a brief tenure as a stockbroker, she zeroed in on Xerox as her company of choice. But the company's Dallas facility wouldn't hire her even as a secretary. So she checked around for the temp service the Xerox office used most frequently, signed on there, and told them she was interested only in Xerox assignments. Within weeks, she landed one and soon was offered a full-time job.

Was this a step back from a stockbroker job? Certainly. Did she care? All that mattered was getting her foot in the door. Then you can start forming alliances, developing mentors, and creating opportunities for yourself. "You can't do anything from the outside looking in," she says.

She showed up fifteen minutes before anyone else and stayed later. She finished assignments early and asked for more. In less than a year, she was planning and arranging trade shows as a project manager in trade show logistics.

Eventually, she convinced a former supervisor to hire her as a program manager to organize product development teams. Here, she could get involved in nearly every area of the company's business without changing jobs and earning a reputation as a job-hopper. She learned marketing in launching personal computers and fax machines. She also learned how to mediate conflict and hold effective meetings. "The product always changed and the team changed," she says. "I thought I'd died and gone to heaven."

Mostly, she got an extremely broad perspective on what made the company tick and how that changed with time and business trends.

Her philosophy was also forged by adversity. Within a year after being recruited by Compaq, her division was shuttered and she was laid off. She realized how fragile corporate structures really were.

So when she signed on as director of business development for Recognition International, she was determined to stay attuned to the latest management trends. "You should see the library of business books I have at home," she says. She also listened carefully to influential people at the company to detect any change in corporate direction.

That came in handy at Recognition, which was constantly in flux. When, for instance, she realized that the customer-training program she was asked to turn into a revenue-producing business after one reorganization "wasn't on anybody's agenda," she let it be known she was looking for something else and was asked to manage the absorption of a recently acquired company. Then, when the company created a Xerox-like program management group, which she had been advocating, she pursued the director's job "as if I were applying from outside," sending her résumé to the appropriate managers.

She got that job, but the company subsequently underwent another seismic shift, moving the marketing of major product lines back to individual units and dismantling the program management group. But Ms. Reed's research had already detected management's effort to reconstruct the company's culture. When a consultant was brought in to create a more team-based culture, she volunteered to assist. She trained in his method and was eventually named vice president of organizational development.

Ms. Reed calls herself the one-minute VP. After just five months, she orchestrated her own demotion to director of service marketing. Why? Recognition had just announced that it was taking a $26 million restructuring charge. Support functions, she reasoned, were highly vulnerable. "When you're getting lean and mean, it's no time to be in corporate," she says.

Ms. Reed was also ready for the new business formation trend of the 1990s. Knowing that corporate life was growing increasingly uncertain, she negotiated a generous severance agreement as part of her self-created demotion. She also hit the books again—both informally (she read about fifty books related to starting your own business) and formally (she took classes). She wanted to learn everything she could about marketing, curriculum development, and personality testing.

When the unexpected happened—the acquisition of Recognition by Banc Tec—and most of the so-called Recognoids were fired, Ms. Reed was ready to go. "I was so happy I had the foresight and the gumption to negotiate that contract," she says. She used it to start her own business as a trainer and consultant in building corporate teams.

B*e alert to new directions; anticipate, prepare, then make your move. The worst that can happen often may not be so bad.*

25

THE RETURN OF THE LIVING DEAD: COMING BACK FROM A DEMOTION

You've just been demoted, and it doesn't feel good. You're embarrassed. *What will my colleagues think? What will my family think?* You're also afraid. *What will become of me?* Finally, you're angry. *How could they do this to me?*

Few events are more demoralizing than a demotion. It calls into question your competence and raises fears for your future. And unlike a firing, a demotion forces you to linger on, as the ghost of Christmas past.

But demotions aren't terminal events. You can recover, if you have the determination and self-awareness to make needed changes—or the wisdom to accept the change you've been handed. In truth, a demotion is often nature's way of telling you you're in the wrong job. Sometimes people even bring it on themselves as a subconscious way of extricating themselves from a bad spot.

Take the most common case of a great individual performer whose personality is totally unsuited to management. He doesn't want the hassle or the internal politics; he hates the daily responsibility and doesn't want to deal with others' problems. Yet he takes the job—for the money, for the prestige, or because it's expected. Some people nevertheless do well but aren't happy. Many others fail miserably.

Modern times brought us the seemingly no-fault, structural demotion. That's like a managerial game of musical chairs. The company restructures, several chairs are removed, and you and a few other unfortunates are left without a seat.

Ann Meier found herself on the wrong end of a corporate shake-up in the early 1990s. After twelve years as head of the training department for an Orlando, Florida, resort company, Ms. Meier found herself without a chair and, in the then tight job market, was forced to accept a lesser position—the nonmanagerial job of program designer for Red Lobster Restaurants, then a General Mills division.

To bolster her self-esteem, she volunteered for meaningful projects that would showcase her skills. "If you're leading a project, you can use all the skills you used running a department," she says.

Ex-managers also worry about whether they can still do the job as an individual contributor. Managing others can have a corrosive effect on your own skills and expertise. Have you fallen behind others in your old area of expertise? Are you still capable of meeting tight deadlines under pressure? Has new technology passed you by? "You'll find a lot of managers whose computer skills aren't as good as those of the people working for them," Ms. Meier says.

Hopefully, you've prepared for that eventuality by keeping up your individual skills and expertise; if not, get thee to night school and industry seminars. Pore over the latest industry intelligence. Pick the brains of peers you respect.

Next, clear the air with your boss. Your presence is undoubtedly an awkward one, and you need to make it clear that you've adapted to your new circumstance and won't be a cancer in the department. Define the boundaries of your new domain; your boss is bound to wonder if you can be a team player. You need to reassure her from the start. Ms. Meier especially wanted to make sure there was a clear-cut line of authority. "When can I make the decision, and when do you need to be involved?" she says.

And don't forget to do some soul-searching. You may not think the demotion was warranted, but somebody did, and you need to know why. Question those who were involved. Was it performance related or political, or a combination of both? Did your style rub higher-ups the wrong way? Or did you fail to win over your staff? Finally the biggest question: What can I do to fix it?

Admittedly, it may be extremely difficult to put Humpty-Dumpty back together again at that same company. That kind of baggage isn't easy to lose. Whether you stay or move on, though, it's important to understand the obstacles you're facing. Too many of us exist in a state of denial about our shortcomings, and that's a surefire way to compound the problems created by a demotion.

Handled with grace and a dose of introspection, a demotion can offer unexpected opportunities to refocus your career.

26

JOB-HOPPING:
ROAD TO RICHES OR RUIN?

Julia Hartman insists that the stigma attached to job-hopping has vanished. Ms. Hartman had better hope so; at last count, the marketing executive had held ten jobs in fifteen years.

Rick Abraham begs to differ. The business development executive found that the five jobs he held in five years quickly became a major sticking point in job interviews. "They say, 'Why should we hire you? How do we know you'll be committed to the job?'"

And so the debate rages on. The answer, as always, is: It depends. Repeat after me, for the umpteenth time: There are no hard-and-fast golden rules to live by in the career game. What is meaningless to one hiring manager is a major red flag to another.

Certainly, in recent years, some managers have become more accepting of candidates whose résumés read like a rock group's world tour. Of course, they haven't had much choice. In a golden age of start-ups and economic expansion, there are just too many jobs and not enough talented managers to go around. To fill a major job, companies often have to raid the managerial ranks of rivals, tossing around bonuses and perks like confetti. And because of that, job-hopping has become an epidemic.

The unprecedented wave of mergers, downsizings, outsourcing, and temping has also served to add multiple lines to managers' résumés in recent years.

At the same time, many companies became enthralled with the idea of pushing broad change in their ranks. That usually meant bringing in someone from outside with a fresh perspective. Suddenly, hiring managers became suspicious of people who stayed in the same organization for too long. What was wrong with them? Why weren't they in demand? Would they be too set in their ways to adapt to our incredibly vital, fast-changing culture? (Corporate self-delusion knows no bounds.)

But the management ranks teem with people from different generations, with different concepts about job-hopping. To some, it remains a sign of lack of commitment and loyalty, an indication that the candidate cares more for money and perks than anything else.

So let's assume for a moment that in the current climate, a certain amount of job-hopping is inevitable and perhaps even desirable. It shows that you're adaptable and have been exposed to a wide variety of management styles and corporate cultures.

But how do you counter the perception that you're a corporate mercenary?

It's important, for example, to develop reasons behind your moves. Show that you weren't just moving around laterally for a bump in salary but were making reasoned decisions to better yourself. Explain what new skills and knowledge you were aiming to pick up with each move; indicate how you took on more responsibility with each move.

You can also turn a possible negative into a positive by describing the differences between the various companies and how you've distilled the best ideas into your own style. "You can show how you did well in this culture and that culture and how adaptable you are," says Mr. Abraham, vice president of business development for Locus Direct Marketing Group, which manages corporate marketing campaigns.

You'll also be asked to explain why you left each job. Reasons that soothe include the desire to stretch, a chance to run your own show, a chance to fill out your trick bag of skills. Bad answers include just wanting more money, couldn't get along with the boss or staff, didn't like the way the company did things, and so forth.

Mr. Abraham has left jobs for a variety of reasons. The company faltered or a project ended or he grew bored and sought new challenges. "I have a lot of curiosity about what's happening in technology and marketing and want to be in the forefront of it," he says.

Still, he admits that his résumé makes him "cringe." Says he: "My choice would be to find a company and stay there the rest of my career."

While his breadth of experience certainly would be an asset in business development, he understands the nervousness about his past. "Nobody wants to hire a VP of business development who's going to develop all these relationships and then leave," he says. "You can do a lot of damage to the company."

Nevertheless, he realizes that if "you're in a position where you can't grow through more responsibility or technical knowledge, you have to think about a change."

If you've come to that point, it helps to know the career profiles of the companies recruiting you. Job-hopping is more commonplace in labor-strapped, creative, and technology-based industries but frowned upon in more traditional businesses, such as financial services.

Ms. Hartman, director of marketing and sales for Mercantile Software, a database marketing company in Piscataway, New Jersey, contends that companies aggressively seeking change are happy hunting grounds for job-hoppers, particularly those with lofty career ambitions. "It's a bold career strategy for people who are really going for it," she says.

For them, this is a planned strategy. Ms. Hartman, for example, decided she wanted to be the top marketing officer for a major corporation, an extravagant dream for someone who started her career as a violinist. To acquire the needed skills, she raced through an MBA and a series of jobs, contract posts, and consulting assignments to gain, as quickly as possible, a broad knowledge of business and management. She eventually distilled her process into her own book: *Strategic Job Jumping—Fifty Very Smart Tactics for Building Your Career.*

"If you change jobs within an industry, you get a 360-degree view of that industry," she says, "so you may be best qualified to see future opportunities and transform a firm to capitalize on those opportunities."

She carries with her a work portfolio, which includes a presentation about marketing campaigns she mounted and excerpts from various reports and presentations she developed. If employers still question her frequent moves and her commitment, she responds: "On the contrary, I get passionately involved in my jobs, because I've made a conscious choice to come to this company at this time for this assignment. This is the assignment I'm choosing for my career."

Whatever your story line, it's critical to line up good references who will ease the hiring manager's concerns about your vagabond career. In the end, that manager wants to hear from someone with firsthand knowledge that he or she won't regret putting you on the payroll.

Job-hopping doesn't carry the stigma it once had, but it is still critical that you be able to explain why frequent job changes made sense and will ultimately benefit your next prospective employer.

27

How to Survive Your Midlife Crisis

No matter how skilled and savvy you are in your career, no matter how fascinating and cutting edge your work now is, it will someday happen: You will roll out of bed, wonder what you're doing with your life, and think about making a change.

Few things are as certain as middle-aged angst, that dreaded feeling that somehow life has passed you by or you've simply missed it somehow.

You question your choices, bemoan your current circumstances, and agonize over the future. You start thinking about hair plugs and working out more. You have a sudden urge to trade in the old car for a racy new model or the old wife for a racy new supermodel.

But more often than not, your agonizing centers around your job. You've always hated it, or you once loved it but there's no challenge anymore. You've plateaued, you're bored, you hate the boss or the wunderkind who just zipped by you on the organizational chart. You want to dump that vice presidency to run a bar in Mazatlán. After all, life is short and getting shorter by the day, and you realize you are closer to the end of your career than the beginning.

Here's where some of the career advisers out there go a little haywire, pushing people into radical career shifts, urging them to find their "bliss." I remember watching as the leader of a group career guidance session, sponsored by a service that shall go unnamed, cajoled one attendee—a man who seemed quite happy working as a manager for a computer retailing company and who, in fact, seemed justifiably proud of the coveted promotion he had just earned—to scrap it all because she saw his face light up when he talked about playing the guitar as a kid. Whoa, Nelly. For all she knew, the guy may have been a lousy guitarist. And not every fanciful dream of youth is worth pursuing, despite the malarkey pushed by TV movies of the week. For a thirtyish guy with a family, the suggestion was, in my mind, outrageous.

The idea of a radical career shift holds a powerful appeal to those in the throes of a middle-aged crisis, and certainly these seismic shifts do work for some. But let's face it: You've spent your whole life building up skills and expertise; that's your career currency, and it's usually far more valuable in the industry you're already in.

Now, I recognize that some gung-ho Boy Scouts out there are shaking their heads, certain they won't fall prey to this dire condition. They're too enthusiastic, and their work is too vital. If they even smell some angst in the neighborhood, they'll just pop another motivational tape into their Walkman and keep on truckin'. Fine. They can skip this chapter. For the other 99 percent of us, here are some tales from the midst of the morass to help shake us from our doldrums and get us moving again.

For twenty-seven years, Richard Dahlberg toiled for Massachusetts Financial Services. Then, when the company wouldn't assign him more staff so that he could aggressively push for growth in the mutual funds he managed, he decided he needed a change of scenery.

But what to do after residing so long at one address? Mr. Dahlberg decided to stay within his sphere of knowledge, the financial services industry. After looking at posts in two banks and a mutual fund, Mr. Dahlberg got an offer to be chief investment officer in the equity asset management group at Salomon Bros. It wasn't a sure bet. Equity management had always been a poor stepchild at Salomon, representing at that time just $1 billion of the firm's $13 billion under management. Mr. Dahlberg wondered how committed Salomon would be to the relatively new business. He also worried about the fact that Salomon was just coming off a run of trading scandals and financial setbacks. And at fifty-five years of age, he would be giving up a secure position where he had been quite successful. In the previous ten years, he had built Massachusetts Financial's balanced fund assets to $4.5 billion from $215 million. "I could have stayed where I was for another ten years and enjoyed the annuity," he says.

Don Crosbie, by contrast, simply walked away from his job as chief financial officer of Dallas-based InterVoice, because he needed a rest after ten intense years of helping to build the telecommunications start-up. "I did some consulting, some sailing, tried to figure out what I wanted to do with my life," he says.

He spent a year flirting with investing in some companies and going on a few job interviews before he decided to form ComVest Partners, an investment research boutique. The idle time didn't worry him, he insists. He has an explorer's mentality, requiring new and exhilarating experiences. "You don't always know where you're going to end up," he says. "There's always some uncertainty, but in my mind, if you have the confidence, a door will open for you."

In contrast with Mr. Dahlberg, he believes that trying to forge a new career while immersed in the old one usually doesn't work. "You end up getting trapped," he says.

While Mr. Crosbie would appear to have made a radical break, closer scrutiny reveals that his new job trades on his well-developed financial analysis skills. "It wasn't as if I were going to be an astronaut," he says.

Many midlifers, fearful that opportunities will dwindle with age, grab the first job that seems to offer change. Take your time and "evaluate a number of situations," Mr. Dahlberg advises. "You have to find the right fit for you."

If you want a more dramatic change, you have to do something drastic.

After sixteen years in the building materials business, Hoyt Gier was uneasy. The senior sales executive was paid well, enjoyed his job, and figured he had a reasonable shot at the CEO post. But, "I went to work for a Canadian firm, which was bought by Belgians, which was bought by Germans," he says. "I didn't want to wake up at fifty with someone in Brussels or Heidelberg or Seattle deciding our unit made no sense; that petrified me."

But he wondered how marketable he would be. "I worked for different companies, but to someone outside the industry, it would look as if I'd been doing the same thing my whole career," he explains. So, at age forty, he quit his six-figure job in Seattle and schlepped his wife and three young children to Hanover, New Hampshire, and Dartmouth's Amos Tuck School of Business for an MBA. It cost him about $250,000 in tuition and lost income, which he paid for by selling his Redmond, Washington, home. The move puzzled his bosses, he says. Even his parents questioned his judgment.

In industries such as investment banking and consulting, the MBA is practically a required entry card for those with management ambitions —especially for those coming from completely different backgrounds. As Mr. Gier notes, "You simply can't get from where I started to where I am going without coming through here." Or someplace like it. He adds: "To break into something completely different, you have to do something to catch someone's attention."

Is an MBA a panacea for middle-aged managers foundering in a sea of uncertainty? Is this the way for them to overcome the reluctance of companies to invest in managers with gray hair who command six-figure incomes?

Of course not.

Some lack the inclination to return to an intense school program at such an advanced age. In some industries, also, the degree would provide only a marginal benefit. Before making such a precipitous and expensive leap, study the backgrounds of the people who are successful in your company or industry of choice. Are they MBA holders? What gaps exist between their experiences and skills and yours, and are there simpler and less expensive ways to fill those gaps?

Still, for managers seeking a midcourse correction, MBAs mean exposure to a wider range of possibilities and a widely accepted credential. With high demand for MBA holders, companies start recruiting early. In his second week of classes, Mr. Gier recalls presentations by Ford, Microsoft, Dell, and Morgan Stanley. He soon discovered the world of private client services.

It was just the kind of relationship-driven business he wanted. Following a summer internship with Goldman, Sachs, he accepted the firm's offer of full-time employment after graduation. He couldn't be happier about it. "Tuck exposed me to many business possibilities new to me or previously thought to be out of reach," he says. "The business world looks a lot bigger to me now than it did just a couple of years ago."

Throughout his transition, Mr. Gier's age wasn't as much of an issue as he feared. Interviewers never mentioned it directly, choosing instead to ask how he would feel working with or reporting to a twenty-seven-year-old. "My response was, 'If I didn't think I could run with these people in the workforce, I wouldn't have come here,'" Mr. Gier says.

Still, he acknowledges that his path isn't for everybody. The tough, competitive environment of the school—he worked late most nights on group projects—is exhausting. And if you can't land in one of the better schools, he advises, forget it. "An <u>MBA</u> from a top school opens doors other MBAs do not," he says.

Further, he says, don't go if you're satisfied with your job, your career path, your company's prospects, and your opportunities to advance and find challenging assignments. Don't go if you're convinced other companies, inside your industry and out, will gladly pay for your skills and experience. Finally, he says, don't go if you don't have the total support of your spouse. This kind of change isn't for the risk averse.

When the itch to change careers strikes, be careful how hard you scratch. Finding a new path in the same industry lets you use some of the career currency you've accumulated. Leaping into an entirely new field can be both risky and expensive.

28

CAN YOU GO HOME AGAIN?

Can you go home again?

It's one of the hoariest myths in the pantheon of career mythology: Once you've left a job, for whatever reason, you are no longer considered loyal or trustworthy by that employer. Returning to the scene of this heinous crime can only result in career disaster.

Nonsense!

The truth is, this kind of thing happens all the time, mainly because managers trying to fill a critical job prefer the devil they know to the devil they don't know. Managers hire the people with whom they feel most comfortable; it's that simple. And unless you jilted his daughter or embezzled company funds during your first visit, his familiarity with you gives you a big edge.

Your chances for success are also enhanced because you know the company's operations, the unwritten rules, the culture. You can hit the ground running.

What reluctance existed among companies has vanished in this market. First, there's that pesky talent shortage. Second, there's the hair trigger companies have developed for managers who shepherd lagging operations. With the need to deliver results quickly paramount, people who already know the drill have a big advantage.

The fabulous flameouts of hotshot outsiders who came roaring into companies only to instantly clash with the culture have also helped to improve the image of corporate retreads.

Sometimes companies recycle former executives as a stopgap to handle a specific project or bridge the gap between generations of managers. That was the case a few years back when PepsiCo tapped its former president, Andrall E. Pearson, as chairman and CEO of the restaurant company it was about to spin off. His assignment: Win over Wall Street prior to a public offering and groom his successor.

But companies are also pursuing young former managers for longer terms. In 1991, Rayna Brown left Ziff-Davis in New York for a plum job at Capitol Records and the chance to be near her family in Los Angeles. But she maintained cordial relations with her former Z-D bosses, and when a new regime took over at Capitol, her former employer welcomed her back and even allowed her to remain on the West Coast.

This doesn't mean that your return engagement will necessarily do boffo business or that you should automatically jump at the chance.

First, remember why you left in the first place. Amid the flattery of a big-bucks offer from a former employer, people will forget the career abuses that initially drove them out. Was there an abusive boss who still wields clout at the company? Was the company slow to promote or otherwise recognize your contribution? And the biggest question: Is there any reason to believe things have changed?

In weighing her return, Ms. Brown listed her abilities and interests and matched them against the company's profile. She eventually opted to return, deciding that she missed the atmosphere and people at Ziff-Davis.

That's another thing about returning. Often, people who leave find the grass on the other side of the fence brown and fetid. Having experienced life from "both sides now," as Joni Mitchell sang, they return with a new appreciation for the old pop stand and renewed enthusiasm.

Andrew Beaver dumped Deutsch Inc. in 1994 when the New York advertising agency was mired in a power struggle. But after just eight months, he decided he was a misfit at Foote, Cone & Belding and jumped at the chance when Deutsch asked him to return to a higher post.

He did, however, first check with former allies at the company. They told him he had to mend some fences with Deutsch executives. That merely meant reassuring the agency chief that his departure hadn't been a statement of support for the chief's since vanquished rival in the power struggle.

"Look at the management team and what your relationships were," he advises. "Who were your advocates, and where are they now?"

Further, don't be seduced by a big bump in salary. The company may be looking for a quick fix and nothing more. What are the company's long-term prospects and your long-term prospects within that structure? How important to the company's overall fortunes is the operation you'll be shepherding? In other words, do you have a reasonable shot at success and desirable career rewards if you deliver?

"Get it all out on the table," Ms. Brown says.

Find other retreads. If there aren't any, that should tell you something right there. If there are, find out how they were treated on their return, whether they've been promoted or shuttled to some satellite operation that contributes 2 percent of the company's sales. If the company doesn't have a reputation for moving people around and promoting from within, "I would look suspiciously at the offer," Ms. Brown says.

If you decide the stars are properly aligned for your return, remember that in your absence, there have inevitably been changes, so your first chore is to catch up. Although she was gone only a year, Ms. Brown returned to a company with new markets and management. "I had to reconnect with all the team managers at the company and get a sense of how things had evolved and what was happening in the market," she says.

Be sure to also reconnect with old friends and allies. You may need them, because there may be pockets of resentment about your return. The resentful must also be addressed head-on; solicit their opinions and recognize their contributions.

Before you decide to go back home, check out the old homestead to see what has changed. Are your old friends still there? How about your old enemies? The last thing you want when you go home is to find nasty surprises.

29

USING A JOB HIATUS
TO BUILD A NEW CAREER

Remember that stuff I was telling you earlier about how managers hate big gaps in a résumé? Why would a strong job candidate have such a gap? they wonder. What's wrong with this picture?

Most managers will tell you that any period of unemployment over a year means, as Ricky Ricardo said, "you've got some 'splainin' to do."

So how about an eleven-year gap? That was the length of the job hiatus taken by Fran Laserson from Moody's Investor Services. But in that time, Ms. Laserson developed new skills, enabling her to move her career in a completely new direction once she returned.

In 1984, Ms. Laserson was forced to leave her job as a bond analyst for Moody's for health and family reasons. At the time, she was an assistant vice president and manager of Moody's midwestern regional ratings group, as well as one of twelve corporate officers on the committee that rates public bonds. "It took me almost a year to get over not working at Moody's," she says.

But in her case, unemployed didn't mean idle. Maybe she couldn't make the time and emotional commitment to a full-time career, but she could stay active in part-time ventures. She served on the board of her alma mater, Sweet Briar College in Virginia. She was president of the women's association of Brick Presbyterian Church. She worked with New York City Parents in Action, a drug abuse program for kids, and she raised funds for the New York Junior League.

These weren't casual volunteer assignments; Ms. Laserson became deeply involved at each organization. At times, she was working longer hours than she had at Moody's. But unlike a full-time career, these volunteer assignments allowed her to cut back when she needed to.

Moreover, she says, the work was in some ways more valuable than some of her for-profit experiences. "You have the ability to get more responsibility," she says. "There was no bureaucracy. I dealt with advertising agencies, led focus groups, learned public relations techniques, evaluated products, created strategic partnerships."

At her church group, she managed a six-figure annual budget and ran the church's annual fund-raiser. At Sweet Briar, she spent two years traveling, talking with donors, and making presentations on behalf of the scholarship fund. She also headed a two-year effort that resulted in a new marketing plan for the small women's school.

For example, instead of flooding prospective students with mail, she set up a telemarketing operation manned by students to illustrate the school's cozy personal touch. Another time, a donor expressed interest in stimulating others to give, so she created Sweet Briar's first matching grant program. "I learned about marketing from hands-on experience at the college," she says. "You have to assess the environment, narrow your target market, develop products, and monitor the market."

The experiences were eye-opening. She notes: "To people in the same boat, I'd say well-chosen nonprofit work is not idle time; it can really be superior on-the-job training for your next career."

As her excitement and successes grew, she started to rethink her career ambitions. "I think it comes back to what comes naturally," she says. "I was a sociology major, so I have an interest in human behavior. What is marketing? It's changing people's behavior." But without the time off to reflect, she believes, she probably wouldn't have made the change.

By 1994, as her terms at nonprofit groups expired, she began to plot the resumption of her career, viewing it as a marketing project. Approaching Moody's as if she were a first-time job seeker, she presented a new résumé that stressed functional skills instead of jobs held. "I thought to myself, If I was hiring someone, what would I be interested in?" she says. "I would want to see skills and expertise." The résumé also shows a marketer's grasp of current hot buttons, such as managing change. "You will see 'change agent' written all over my résumé," she says.

Moody's was apparently impressed, hiring her as a marketing consultant. Within six months, she was named vice president of strategic marketing programs. She later took on additional marketing duties when Moody's, in a reorganization, combined the corporate and public finance departments.

There are several steps people can take to minimize damage to their careers from a lengthy hiatus. Consider part-time work or working from home—anything that keeps you in touch with your industry and allows you to keep your job skills sharp. Consider returning to school for an advanced degree or taking classes to add, say, computer skills. You don't want to be out-of-date with your profession when you return.

Maintain professional ties. If you've left on good terms, with the intention of returning, ask to be kept on the company's mailing list for memos and newsletters, and attend company social events. Ms. Laserson kept up with changing issues through professional associations.

The lesson here is that unemployment doesn't have to mean stagnation. If you're faced with a long period away from work, use the time productively to maintain old skills, develop new ones, and reflect on the direction you want your career to take.

How badly a long gap in a résumé hurts you will depend on what you were doing during that period—and how persuasively you can explain it.

PART FIVE

Swimming in a Sea of Change: Fight or Flight?

30

THE HIGH-ANXIETY, LOW-SELF-ESTEEM BLUES

In careers, as in blackjack, it's never easy to admit that it's time to cash in your chips and move on, even if you're on a horrendous losing streak. Surely the cards will turn your way soon. You can't have such bad luck forever, can you?

In either game, that's dangerous thinking. But at least in blackjack, you know that no matter what happens with your current lousy hand, you will get a fresh deal in five minutes. In your career, you may have to play the hand you are dealt for some time.

Still, it's so difficult to give up on a job and start that long, lonely search for a new one. Believe me, I've been there, and so have a few million of your brethren. You've committed a lot of time, energy, and effort in your current position and are reluctant to give up on it. Besides, the thought of suffering the thousands of little indignities awaiting you in the hated job-hunting process has you thinking: Maybe this situation isn't so bad after all. Better the devil you know, right?

Certainly, some apparent dead ends can be averted by reinventing your job or creating a new one (see the next two chapters for more on that). Unfortunately, most bad situations just don't get better, and sooner or later you're going to have to overcome your self-doubts and inertia and hurl yourself into the abyss.

Before you do, however, make sure you're reading the political tea leaves correctly. Is the problem the job, the boss, or you? I know it's heresy to suggest that the blame for career malaise may lie with you and isn't the result of a thickheaded, tyrannical boss or a dysfunctional organization. But we're talking about truth and reality here. We all know, deep in our heart of hearts, exactly where blame for your career yips often resides.

Have you really tried to understand the company's needs and your boss's point of view? Are your ambitions leading you into an adversarial position with your boss instead of a supportive one? Have you really put maximum effort into your work?

If you can honestly answer yes to those questions, you may have a real problem. But how can you tell that it's time to move on? Here are the telltale signs that you've reached a dead end in your current job:

• **Has your job or department slipped out of the company's mainstream?** "A dead giveaway that it is time to move on to a new position is when you have no voice mails and your in-box is regularly empty," says Michael Farrow, who feared that his job as manager of finance for a division of a giant entertainment company was no longer central to the company's future.

The job once dealt with critical, revenue-generating issues but later focused largely on the less cherished expense side. "You want to be involved in things that people care about," he says.

• **Are you mired in a political quagmire?** Brian Silverstein, an actuary at a major benefits consulting firm, was promoted to a highly visible team working on a new product. But a year later, he says, the product was languishing and team members were bickering over crumbs of available work.

As the junior member of the team, Mr. Silverstein was squeezed out of assignments, had no real authority, and chafed at the managers' habit of parceling out miserly bits of information on a need-to-know basis. Worse, he was getting little practical experience and he started retreating from taking initiative because it was "too much of a headache to fight team members," he recalls.

• **Are you getting undeserved lukewarm performance reviews?** No doubt about it, someone is building a case against you. At most companies, that's the primary function of the review process, in spite of high-minded talk about career development.

• **Have you been bypassed for more than one promotion?** Getting nosed out for one job is understandable; if it's becoming a habit, you should be getting the message that you've shifted from the fast track to a rural milk run.

• **Are you being shut out of critical decisions and meetings?** The old freeze-out is a common tactic by cowardly managers who can't confront you with their dissatisfaction. Instead, they try to make you so uncomfortable, you'll leave on your own. It's a long, painful process for everyone involved.

• **Are you getting insulting raises—or worse, no raises?** That's another freeze-out tactic, usually trotted out if the more subtle ones fail to reach your synapses.

• **Are your responsibilities and budget being reduced?** This could be part of an operation slipping out of the mainstream. But it could also be a sign that the powers-that-be have lost confidence in you. Either way, it's time to move to something else.

• **Do you feel a chill when you're around peers or superiors?** Politically astute colleagues can smell a decomposing career carcass and start walking the other way when you approach. If your office conversations are becoming perfunctory and old acquaintances are being forgot, you're toast.

• **Are you getting bored?** Sometimes you just outgrow a job. It's no longer challenging, or you become intrigued by some new line of business that seems more vital and growing.

As she watched numerous colleagues leave for greener pastures, Elizabeth Alvarez feared she had stayed at her company too long. Even though she was getting added responsibilities, she felt she was missing out on better opportunities.

Many experience this fear, especially when talent-short companies are raiding each other shamelessly, tossing around glossy new titles, big raises, and signing bonuses.

If you leave, make sure it's for the right reasons. The money may be great, but if you're not getting new responsibilities and increased authority, if you're not moving into a situation where you feel comfortable with your employer and your immediate bosses, you will quickly grow dissatisfied again.

Don't make a hasty decision, but if the signs of decay are unmistakable, don't wait for the disposal team to arrive. Leave on your terms; it makes for a better story in future job interviews.

31

REINVENTING YOUR JOB

Should you determine that your career progress has come to a screeching halt, leaving isn't your only option. Some problems are repairable. If you like what you're doing for the most part and prospects for advancement remain viable, you owe it to yourself to give it a shot. After all, who's to say the next job will be any better or will even last long enough for you to find the rest rooms?

So get ready; we're going to negotiate a better job with your boss. Bah, you say. That's not the way things are done around here. Oh, what a tired lament. Besides, at this point, what have you got to lose?

Here's the plan, step by step:

• **Figure out what you want.** What would make your job better? What would make you want to come to work in the morning?

Sometimes a small adjustment can yield big results. Susan Taylor, once a clerk in Amoco's microfilm department in Calgary, Alberta, was surprised to learn, through an evaluation made by an outside training firm, that what she really wanted was simple: more recognition from her boss. After discussing it with her manager, Ms. Taylor started getting more positive strokes, grew happier in her work, and was eventually promoted to staff assistant.

Don't ask for things you can't get or aren't capable of doing, however. You may want a promotion, but are you willing to do what's necessary to get it?

• **Schedule a meeting with your boss.** Don't wait for your annual performance review. This is a separate subject, and it's your show, not your manager's.

• **Ask your boss to analyze your skills and potential.** There's little use arguing for greater responsibility if your boss is convinced you can't handle it. You must know where you stand.

• **Present your own views**. Don't argue; offer examples of things you've accomplished. Emphasize achievements you think the boss may have overlooked or forgotten. Segue into the ways you'd like your job to change. Negotiate new duties and goals and ways to measure your success in reaching those goals. Some people draw up a formal contract on those issues.

• **Go for it.** Once your plan is in place, pursue it aggressively. This is also the time to initiate new projects that will get your boss's attention and bring you into contact with key managers and customers.

• **Don't expect radical change immediately.** Chuck Cartier, a senior regional manager at Johnson & Johnson's LifeScan division, learned that his boss wanted him to develop more polished managerial skills before considering him for the area sales manager job he coveted. It took time, as Mr. Cartier took American Management Association courses to improve his leadership and strategic planning skills, then returned to burnish his finance and communications abilities.

It took a year, but he got the promotion.

Reinventing your job may not always work; it requires an open-minded boss and an employee who is part negotiator and part diplomat. If it does work, however, it can revitalize your career with much less upheaval than searching for a new job.

Don't wait for your boss to reinvent your job for you. Take the upper hand by identifying ways that changing your job will benefit the company, then don't be shy about pushing for change.

32

CREATING YOUR OWN NEW JOB

Your job stinks, and it isn't going to smell any nicer in six months. You could bail out, or, as we have seen, you could negotiate new terms for your present job.

How about creating your own new job, drawn up to your specifications? Can't be done, you say?

Joe DeMeyer did it. Feeling underutilized at Keithley Instruments, the software engineer proposed a new position directing software development and got the new post.

David Morrison did it, too. He sought to free himself from a desk-bound manager's job at Toronto Dominion Bank and sold his bosses on the idea of making him the official corporate trend spotter.

Betsy Blair, a Dell Computer sales manager, saw a job that wasn't being done and did it. Thus, she created the position of communications liaison, which basically bridged the gap between sales and manufacturing, then she sold the idea to superiors.

So it can be done. I'm not saying it's easy, and it isn't for the faint of heart. Many a lunk-headed manager may turn a deaf ear to such a radical proposal or withhold the support needed to make the new position work. Even so, they've got to notice your ambition and innovative nature.

But if companies are serious about promoting change and having employees act like owners, they should welcome this kind of thinking.

All three of our featured performers could have gone elsewhere for a fresh challenge. Instead, they studied their organizations' needs and matched them with their own set of skills to create new jobs.

Here's how they did it:

After eleven years at Keithley, which makes electricity measurement instruments, Mr. DeMeyer wanted to advance from developing software to directing its development. To bolster his bid, he earned an MBA in his spare time. But he was blocked by performance reviews that criticized his frequent pursuit of his own design ideas rather than those of his manager. That wasn't a particularly deft career strategy; constantly ignoring the boss's ideas rarely leads to promotions.

Nevertheless, he took his idea to a senior executive, who asked for more details. Preparing a detailed plan is critical to the job creation process. It tells whoever reads it that you've put a lot of thought into it and, hopefully, demonstrates your grasp of the company's needs. It also gives your boss ammunition with which to argue at the next level.

Mr. DeMeyer, who got the job six months later, says his global view was responsible. "When all this started, I was looking at a single subdepartment with very little prospects," he says. "The leap I made was when I asked, 'Could I do this for the whole department?' That's what worked for me."

After four years at Dell, Betsy Blair saw a critical problem: Sales reps promised deliveries with little knowledge of manufacturing's ability to keep those promises. She felt she could bridge the gap. Although she felt she might lose some career momentum by abandoning the sales career track, she felt the job would broaden her knowledge and prepare her for a general management position.

It worked. After fourteen months she was promoted to a program director's post, and the job she created still exists.

Ms. Blair advises job creators to brush up on their presentation skills. "In the beginning, I was selling it to a lot of senior executives," she says. "After I started the job, I had to sell it to my peers."

Having lost a promotion to a younger fast tracker, Mr. Morrison confronted his dissatisfaction with his job as manager of corporate training. What he really liked was public speaking, a skill he had developed to overcome a stammer. And when he spoke at business conferences, he picked up valuable intelligence on business trends. His report to bank management about growing customer demand for better product delivery, for example, helped push efforts to expand and improve the bank's customer services.

Why not formalize the role he was already filling in his spare time? "There was a realization that an organization our size could use somebody who gets out in the world and finds out what's going on," he said.

He was offered a year to prove the position's value. More than a decade later, he has been promoted twice and is currently vice president of human resources development.

There are common threads in these three tales. All had some personal goal in mind. But if that was as far as it went, none would have convinced management to go along with their scheme. They sold the idea based on their grasp of the company's needs and their ability to persuade management that the jobs they were creating were critical to the company.

It won't work any other way.

To create a new job for yourself, know your company and know yourself; spot needs where no one thought they existed before.

33

SHOULD YOU TAKE A BUYOUT AND GO BYE-BYE?

What should you do if the company offers you a buyout?

By doing so, the company has essentially defined you as middle-aged and nonessential.

While that may not jibe with your vision of your self-worth, there's no point in wallowing in angst. And for many, the offer represents opportunity.

Angered by demands to shrink his staff, James Hillestad asked for and accepted an early retirement package from Chemical Bank in 1987. The move freed him to turn a beloved avocation into a successful vocation. If offered a buyout, he advises, "take it and run. The writing is on the wall."

Jack Adjami has a decidedly different point of view. He accepted a buyout in 1994, when he realized his job in IBM's international division was about to be exported to South America. A prolonged period of unemployment ensued, while his colleagues who had rejected the offer seemed secure. An obviously bitter Mr. Adjami says that others facing the decision should stay put, under any circumstances. "Even if they have to work twenty-four hours a day, with expanded job responsibilities," he says.

Few career decisions are more difficult or emotional than whether or not to accept a buyout. The offer usually targets middle-aged middle managers with families, mortgages, and less than stellar job prospects elsewhere. And unless the company has a great 401(k) plan or the manager has invested brilliantly, the proceeds from the offer aren't likely to get him to the end of his days.

On the other hand, once you've been identified as nonessential, what kind of future do you have with that company anyway?

If you receive a buyout offer during your career, here are some questions to ask yourself. And because I'm so helpful, I've even provided the answers:

• **Should I try to negotiate better terms or wait for a sweetened offer?** That's easy: No and no. Buyouts are "take it or leave it" deals. You may be able to negotiate little things, like a slightly later exit date, but the terms aren't going to get any sweeter. In fact, any subsequent offer would likely be for less. Otherwise, why take the first offer?

• **Is the offer fair?** One week's pay per year of service is considered low, three weeks generous. A good package would also include three to five years' credit toward retirement benefits, extension of health benefits at least through the period you're getting the buyout money, and outplacement assistance.

• **Am I a keeper?** If you're over forty, haven't gotten a promotion or significant raise lately, and rank in the top 25 percent of your job category in salary, start worrying. Other clues: How critical is your department and your job to the company? Is there an adequate replacement in the wings? Are you blocking younger executives?

Even if you are a keeper, beware the road ahead. It isn't uncommon for a company to finish the cost-cutting job by following a buyout with a big layoff. How stressful will that be?

If you do stay, expect to crank up your game a notch and perform at higher levels if you want to avoid the deadwood designation.

• **What are my prospects outside the corporate cocoon?** Those under fifty have the best chance of finding comparable work, and the buyout money may carry those over sixty into retirement. Those in between face a tough time. Mr. Adjami was fifty-eight when he left as IBM's transportation marketing manager for Latin

America. In his subsequent unemployment, only a two-year consulting gig kept him going.

He mailed out hundreds of résumés, attended job fairs, and joined Forty-Plus, a support group for unemployed managers of a certain age. But he is being squeezed between experienced consultants with Ph.D.'s and low-cost college graduates. And thirty-three years with a single employer marks him as inflexible to many other employers. "Every morning I go to Forty-Plus," he says. "I sit on the train and the subway, see all those people rushing to work, and think, Why not me?"

• **What do I really want, and what am I prepared for?** The most likely source of jobs these days comes from entrepreneurial companies that could use a few gray hairs sprinkled amid the curly locks and dreadlocks. But if you're a long-term employee with one large company, how much of an entrepreneur are you likely to be? Contract work—often with the old employer—and temporary assignments can buy you time and, for some, can provide sufficient income and excitement. And if you've got some money stashed away, this could be your chance to take a flier on a start-up and the possibility of a big stock option payoff.

Some do adapt. Consider Mr. Hillestad, who was prepared when he quit as Chemical's vice president of creative services. He was already a part-time dealer in collectible toy soldiers, a longtime passion. The three years' salary he received (spread over four years) enabled him to expand the business, buy his dream house in the Pocono Mountains of Pennsylvania, and build a toy soldier museum.

"I wear a suit twice a year," he says proudly. "I eat at the diner. We have eight acres populated with bears and deer; we want for nothing and are free of all the anxieties that go with the corporate environment.

"It's a tough call. All things being equal, in this superheated economy, I'd say take the money and run; it's likely you'll find a comparable job, although there are no guarantees. My best advice? Save diligently and invest wisely; it's the only way to make the decision easier."

Should You Take a Buyout and Go Bye-Bye?

A *buyout offer is a wake-up call: You're expendable. Unless you're prepared to make a substantial commitment to changing that perception, treat it as an opportunity to take the money and run.*

34

WIELDING THE BROOM: WHO GETS SWEPT OUT, THE OLD WAYS OR THE NEW MANAGER?

In the 1990s, the business buzzword became high art, the concept that launched a thousand guru books. And there was no more powerful, compelling buzzword in the entire decade than this one: change agent.

Its mere utterance made gurus quiver and executives drool. The phrase became common verbiage for management job descriptions and one of those keywords that had to appear in your résumé for the screening software to pick up. All of American business wanted someone to come in with a new broom and sweep away the cobwebs of the old corporate culture—making way, I presume, for new cobwebs.

Because it has the aroma of management faddishness, the change agent craze has died down somewhat. But all that means is that managers are looking for different ways to describe it. Scratch beneath the surface of almost any executive job interview at a company whose stock price has dipped a few percentage points and here's what you'll find: "We want someone to come in here and shake things up, someone who can create *real* change."

But if you're one of those managers being interviewed, beware booby traps, because corporate cultures have proven surprisingly resistant to real change and senior management's commitment to change has often withered in the face of internal opposition.

Before you take on one of these new broom assignments, assess the likelihood of success. If signs of change are already turning up around the company, there's a good chance there will be strong support for your measures. The time may be ripe for an overhaul if the chairman has just turned seventy and there's an air of change in the wind anyway.

Roy King weighed all the pros and cons when then slumping IBM came knocking on his door in 1993. As a management consultant with KPMG Peat Marwick and Booz•Allen & Hamilton, he had seen colleagues leave for "change agent" jobs before, only to watch their efforts sputter because of limited support within the company. Many took those jobs because of a strong personal relationship or because the suitor was a client. But that's not enough if the job is defined as a change agent assignment. Without several supporters in top management, Mr. King says, "you can always be viewed as an outsider." If your sponsor leaves, he adds, "you're left hanging there."

IBM wanted Mr. King to play a major role in its restructuring as vice president of worldwide production industries consulting services, a job that involved consulting and selling those consulting services to clients.

After considerable reflection, Mr. King took the job. The financial rewards were great, and the opportunity to switch from advising to real management authority was alluring. And he was convinced IBM was serious about change. After all, the company had just brought in the ultimate change agent, former RJR Nabisco chief Louis Gerstner, as CEO.

The company's commitment is crucial. "If you have to make radical changes, will they be supportive of those changes?" he asks. Fortunately, he felt an instant rapport with Mr. Gerstner, and he had the comfort of knowing Bob Howe, IBM's general manager of financial services and a Booz•Allen alum. "If it wasn't for Bob and his track record, I probably wouldn't have made the move," he says. Mr. Howe provided him with a candid assessment of what had and hadn't worked during IBM's turnaround effort and what challenges remained.

Finally, he got a handshake agreement assuring him of the authority to hire and invest in the operation as he saw fit. "You don't want to have them say, 'You have to make these changes, and oh, by the way, your workforce is being downsized 30 percent,'" he says.

While he probably should have asked for those assurances in writing, Mr. King knew his men. Later, he said, the IBM management "exceeded" his expectations for support.

Once you're in the door, take the temperature of the place. Identify the hardest cases to win over and the general appetite for change. Take it slow, starting with easy-to-sell items and enlisting the aid and expertise of your staff. Change agents aren't bulls in a china shop; they're diplomats and motivators who win support for their ideas through persuasion and trust building.

Whatever you do, though, don't burn your bridges. In many cases, the only thing that gets changed is the change agent, who is swept out to make room for a new one.

Tales abound of executives brought in with promises of support for sweeping reforms, only to find that senior management didn't have the stomach for the turmoil that inevitably accompanies change. Executive recruiter Dennis Krieger, of New York's Seiden Krieger Assoc., tells of the executive imported because the CEO of an industrial distribution company wanted to totally revamp the financial department. He was fired in four months for being "too aggressive and upsetting too many people," Mr. Krieger says.

The executive's boss probably wasn't lying about wanting radical change. That's what most CEOs think they want until one of their pet oxen gets gored or some old-line executives start complaining about the new guy's lack of appreciation for the structure in which they've invested so much of their time and energy. That's when many executives start backtracking.

With hostile—or worse, indifferent—staffs and wavering commitments from top management to contend with, you may find in the end that your best ideas for change involve changing your job and your address.

Creating real change in a company is perilous. Most companies pay lip service to change but retreat in the face of turmoil, while those that really need change probably are already in serious trouble.

35

POSTMERGER TRAUMA:
HOW TO AVOID BEING A DEER
IN THE HEADLIGHTS

Few things can create career angst as quickly as a big corporate merger. Suddenly, all your assumptions about your job and your employer are called into question. What will the new management expect? How do they measure performance? Will the culture change, and will I fit into it? How independent will we be? Most of all, should I start looking for new employment?

Marylyn Rosenblum knows those anxieties well, having experienced it twice. The experiences taught her valuable lessons on what to do and not do during a period of such turmoil.

In 1986, Ms. Rosenblum worked for a book division at CBS that was sold to Harcourt Brace. She ended up leaving and moving her family cross-country to Novato, California, to become vice president of education sales and marketing for Broderbund Software. Lo and behold, in 1994, Broderbund agreed to be acquired by Electronic Arts. After several months of haggling, the deal collapsed.

While it lasted, though, the proposed merger created considerable worry for Broderbund employes. There would be job redundancies and new bosses with whom to contend. "I felt terribly exposed," Ms. Rosenblum says. "It gave you some tiny inkling of what it was like to be a slave; you woke up in the morning and your ownership had changed."

This particular deal also carried with it the potential for a cataclysmic culture clash. Idealistic Broderbund employees worried that Electronic Arts, a maker of commercial video games, wouldn't appreciate their zeal for high-toned educational software for kids.

Ms. Rosenblum felt relatively protected, since educational sales wasn't a strong point for EA. But she knew that everyone was vulnerable in a merger. So she updated her résumé and started listening more intently when management recruiters called. Finding a new job wouldn't have been a big problem, she reasoned. She was in the middle of a red-hot industry, and she had few family restrictions—her husband's antique business was portable. As a sales and marketing person, she also had a wide range of contacts. "I knew I could turn on that switch if I had to," she says.

The experience "changes one's sense of security," she says. "You come in every Monday morning and wonder what's going to happen this week. I don't think that will go away for me."

How do you protect your job in a merger? Just follow my "Career Guide for the Besieged," to wit:

• **Don't prejudge.** Ms. Rosenblum's less than flattering perception of the Electronic Arts corporate culture diminished after meeting with her prospective boss there. She discovered they shared more values than she had expected. "I liked him and felt more comfortable about it," she says.

• **Don't do anything rash.** The deal could fall through. Or it could be completed and turn out to be a great opportunity. Either way, it will take a few months to sort things out. Use the time to plot out what you really want in your job and your career and see if you can get that in these new circumstances. Ms. Rosenblum says that some Broderbund employees jumped ship shortly after the proposed merger was announced. Perhaps they all got great new jobs with little relocation or career trauma, but I suspect some ended up kicking themselves for acting hastily.

• **Do the due diligence dance.** What's your new parent's strategy and style? Which product areas are they most keenly interested in? Which are growing fastest? Which are being phased out? Why did the company buy you? In which parts of your operation are they most and least interested? Does the company need your manufacturing capability or your technical expertise? For your sake, hope for the latter.

• **Make sure you're reading the tea leaves correctly.** Just because the acquiring company doesn't have someone in its organizational chart that does what you do doesn't necessarily mean you are safe. Perhaps the position isn't there because the company doesn't feel it needs someone like you. That would make you one of the first to go.

• **Simplify.** This is a stressful time, so maybe it isn't the right time to buy that third car or the vacation property in Florida. Don't make major, life-altering changes until you've sorted out your career quandary.

• **Don't resist change.** It's easy to see the acquiring company as marauding heathens who don't appreciate your tender sensibilities, but keep an open mind. That knee-jerk hostility dooms many a manager to extinction as soon as the new owners recognize that you're a potential cancer in the new corporate body. Maybe the new guys on the block have something valuable to teach you. Besides, in mergers, as with the Borg (for you *Star Trek* fans), "resistance is futile."

• **Don't play it safe.** After a merger, it's assumed that the new operational plan is set in concrete. But chaos is more often the rule. The merger was done because there was some financial advantage to it; there's rarely a detailed assimilation plan. Most people don't know where they fit or if they fit and end up sitting around waiting for something to happen, for someone to tell them what to do. Those people are just waiting to be lined up and shot. In this chaotic climate, fortune favors the bold. Managers are looking for people with ideas about how this new mix should work and how to implement it. This is your chance to strut your stuff and make a strong first impression.

• **Finally, always be ready to leave.** "If you want loyalty, buy a dog," Ms. Rosenblum says. "I tell people who work for me to take every opportunity to expose themselves to people outside the company so they're in a position to call and say, 'Hey, remember me?'"

The truth is, in any merger, some people are going to leave, voluntarily or otherwise. Are you now redundant? How strong is the position of your counterpart in the acquiring company?

If you're up against the chairman's son or the president's chosen heir apparent, you don't have to bang your head against the wall until it's bloody to know it's time to leave.

Don't make hasty judgments about how a merger might affect you. Others will, and that can give you unexpected opportunities. But be sure your parachute is properly packed.

36

CHASING THE START-UP
POT OF GOLD

If anything has really changed in this so-called new economy, it is our utter fascination and preoccupation with the entrepreneurial life. The opportunity to start your own business has always been with us, but some things happened in the decade preceding the new millennium that suddenly made this the preferred path for a growing number of people who in previous generations would have been climbing a corporate management ladder somewhere.

So what happened?

The downsizing era of the early 1990s, which saw tens of thousands of white-collar workers hurled into the unemployment abyss, broke the bonds of loyalty and security that had tied managers to their corporate families for decades. Women, still frustrated by the slowness of companies to accept them as leaders, were especially driven to start their own companies. Throw in the fact that new technology and, especially, the Internet made it much cheaper to start businesses at the same time that an era of stock market prosperity was freeing up billions of dollars of capital to launch new ventures, and you've got a recipe for a start-up boom.

Then came the cherry on top: the great Internet hype, which turned hordes of young tech pups in sneakers and blue jeans into instant billionaires and titans of industry. Who didn't want to get a piece of that?

The rocket-ship ride ended abruptly when the economy slowed and so many Internet companies were exposed as apparitions. Suddenly, all of those people bolting from comfortable corporate jobs or dropping out of MBA programs in order to cash in started reconnecting with the joys of résumés and interviewing techniques.

Still, dreams die hard. Once released, it's tough to stuff the entrepreneurial genie back into his lamp. But like anything else, entrepreneurism isn't for everybody. So let's try to sort out what it takes in the real world to succeed as your own boss.

To have a chance, entrepreneurs need a clear, long-term idea of the market niche they're pursuing and a short-term willingness to revise or completely scrap that idea on a moment's notice. That's easier said than done for people who often come to business ownership with a long and passionately held idea of the kind of business they want to run. But no matter how good the idea or how much research they've done, entrepreneurs can't become too enamored of their business plan, because market conditions can change so rapidly.

AvantGo, a company that wanted to sell software to transfer corporate web data to handheld devices, quickly learned that its best customers, media companies, didn't want to mess with buying and learning new software—they wanted AvantGo to provide the service instead. So the company, in essence, had to reinvent itself on the fly.

The successful entrepreneur must also be what venture capitalists call a "people magnet," who can attract critically needed talent. Personally, people magnets must be high in self-confidence but low enough in ego to surround themselves with high-powered talent and even to step aside, if it's in the company's best interest. Joe Kraus, one of the founders of Excite Inc., served as its first CEO, pretty lofty stuff for a guy whose previous business experience was delivering pizza. Knowing his limitations, he dove into on-the-job training by rotating among many operating roles, including business development, international development, marketing, and content. But as the industry grew, he recognized that this wasn't enough (don't laugh; some never see that light bulb go on). "If I were a venture capitalist looking at a twenty-three-year-old executive, I'd say, 'Yeah, he's smart, but can he take the company to $1 billion [in sales]? Probably not,'" he says. "You can't build a $1 billion company without someone who has seen what a $1 billion company looks like."

Eventually, he says, every entrepreneur must decide which is more important: success or control. Excite's founding team opted for success and started bringing in what Mr. Kraus calls "adult supervision."

So in 1996, he replaced himself, recruiting George Bell to be CEO and taking the post of senior vice president for business development.

Venture capitalists want people who are intensely committed to the company, not just their careers. "We're looking for the guy who is waking up at night thinking about his company," says Peter Ziebelman, a partner in 21st Century Internet Investment Partners, San Francisco. His firm backed one entrepreneur in part because he was a competitive bike racer, which indicated that he had a fighting spirit.

While the popular image of today's entrepreneur is the computer nerd with a head filled with arcane algorithms, venture capitalists tend to favor people with a sales or marketing background, people who have successfully marketed to similar customers before and who understand the sales cycle. Look at the Internet companies that survived; most did so by creating powerful brands, not because of their nifty technology.

Of course, now that sanity has returned to the market and the brief age of truly easy money has passed, entrepreneurs must brush up on their personal salesmanship (at least those who didn't have the wisdom to sell their stock at the peak). Most important, they must be skilled fund-raisers, capable of delivering a concise, coherent, and compelling message under trying circumstances, without becoming so obsessed with the process that they forget their main responsibility is building a business. In that regard, they must also be willing to brave financial extinction without blinking. Even successful entrepreneurs skate along that edge at some point.

Kevin Klingler, founder of Sonic Desktop Software, Chatsworth, California, calls his experience a "rocky road." The company, which develops software for adding sound tracks to video projects, was founded in 1994 by the former composer of music for TV movies, who got the idea for the start-up while working as a manager for a software company.

He plunged into in-depth market research: patents, market potential, marketing strategies. He even interviewed potential customers,
hoping to get a clear idea of their needs.

Absent a big pile of dough from venture capitalists who think
they're looking at the next Microsoft, most start-ups are launched
with money from friends and relatives and often kept going in the
early stages by personal savings and credit cards. If the business plan is
intriguing enough, they might get seed capital from wealthy investors
known as "angels," a quirky and often secretive bunch who specialize
in the risky but potentially lucrative investment strategy of backing
companies from their inception.

Hopefully, the company will soon be able to demonstrate its
soundness and attract more established venture capital backing that
will sustain it for another year or two. Depending on how much
promise the company displays, it could go through three or four
rounds of funding before going public or otherwise raising enough
capital to become self-sufficient.

Through all this, the budding entrepreneur must repeatedly make
his or her sales pitch—at venture capital conferences, at cocktail parties, and in conference rooms filled with skeptical venture fund partners. You may have anywhere from thirty minutes to just one or two
to deliver your so-called elevator pitch (so-called because sometimes
you must get through it in the time it takes to ride the elevator to
someone's office).

Just don't get bogged down in technical or organizational detail, a
common flaw of new entrepreneurs.

In early pitches for Akamai Technologies, the Cambridge, Massachusetts, Internet infrastructure company, the founders, a group of
MIT types, showed a lot of slides and talked about "consistent batch-
ing," an algorithm that has to do with how data is stored and
retrieved. "We thought, Here are some cool solutions to hard problems," recalls Jonathan Seelig, one of the founders and vice president
of strategy and corporate development. "It turns out, nobody cares
about that; they care about how that turns into something your customer buys."

One of the venture capital firm's partners took them aside. "He
said, 'Okay, this is interesting technology, it sounds like you're smart,

you've got the pedigree that comes from being from MIT. But what are people buying from you, what do they want, what are you going to do with the business?'"

After that, Mr. Seelig says, Akamai's founders became a much more market-focused group. He advises entrepreneurs to concentrate on defining the market and customers they're pursuing, what services they would provide, and the demand for those services. "Venture capitalists want to know how big the opportunity is," he says. And, he adds, they want to hear it in plain English, devoid of industry buzzwords.

No matter how good your idea is and how compelling your pitch, however, there's no escaping the fact that starting your own company is a grinding, pressure-packed gauntlet to be run. The seed funding for Sonic Desktop Software, Mr. Klingler's company, never exceeded six figures. After differences emerged on the company's direction, his backers backed out of a second round. So he focused on building the business instead of raising money, hopeful that he could sign enough deals to fund development and interest investors. He figured he might even have to work elsewhere to pay the bills.

At several stages, Sonic almost capsized. Two big sales kept the company going when angel funding ran out. Mr. Klingler trimmed staff and marketed strictly through advertising to conserve capital until a company agreed to swap marketing expertise for stock. "We just kept going from one deal to the next to the next," he says.

Everyone, of course, has heard the quintessential start-up dream story: Two guys scribble down an idea on a napkin at a burrito stand, some venture capitalist goes ape over it and showers them with millions of dollars to get started, and a year later, the whole grand scheme goes public and makes' everyone millions. It's the tale that keeps everyone dreaming those big dreams and launching those endless numbers of companies.

But Mr. Klingler's story is more typical. And even more commonplace are tales of the folks whose dream crashes—or never even gets off the runway. The majority of start-ups fail. That's a fact. If you can't stand that kind of uncertainty and insecurity, this isn't the life for you.

None of this is meant to discourage your entrepreneurial yearnings, but if you proceed, do so realistically. Are you ready to bootstrap your company with funds you have begged, borrowed, and hopefully not stolen from friends and relatives? Are you ready to empty your savings account and max out your credit cards to meet the payroll in months when cash flow sags? Can you handle the resultant stress? Are you a rainmaker who can close big deals and keep revenues flowing in the early start-up stages, when you don't have much, if any, of a marketing staff? Were you careful not to burn your bridges to the corporate world? Do you have a backup plan in mind if the grand scheme doesn't pan out?

Don't even think of taking a triple gainer into the deep end of the entrepreneurial pool until you have plumbed the depths of your psyche and can honestly answer yes to all those questions.

PART SIX

OFFICE POLITICS: PLAYING WELL WITH OTHERS

37

MASTERING OFFICE POLITICS WITHOUT BECOMING A JERK

I'm always amused when people tell me they don't play office politics. Another variation on that theme is that in the new economy, success comes solely from generating the best ideas; there is neither the time in our eighty-hour workweeks nor the inclination in this rapidly moving meritocracy to participate in anything as petty and banal as office politics.

Yeah, right.

Have you noticed the postings on some of these office gossip websites like the Vault? They're largely a litany of complaints from people working at these icons of the new economy about all the petty office politics they must endure on any given day.

Some things never change. Until robots replace humans, corporate politics, that most human of activities, will endure. Few areas of corporate life are more universally despised—or as ubiquitous—and few have more impact on a manager's career. As long as more people are vying for the corner office than could possibly occupy it, as long as fear, ego, and ambition remain part of human nature, politics will continue to help shape your career.

Oh sure, performance, skills, and knowledge matter, if you want to be picky about it. I'm not cynical enough to pooh-pooh those essential career building blocks. But by the time you've reached a certain managerial level, there's little to choose from among various job or promotion candidates. They've all got credentials and sterling track records and sparkling recommendations from VIPs.

What separates them at that point goes by many names, depending upon which spellbinding guru you're reading at the moment—learning the unwritten rules, emotional intelligence, and so on. They're all code words for that old standby, office politics.

Some will certainly dispute this contention (surprise, surprise), but when you boil these buzzwords down to the basics, they're all about maneuvering within the bounds of your company's culture. And you can do it without becoming a jerk.

Of course, if your idea of office politics is backstabbing rivals, hogging credit, or spreading malicious gossip, well, then, you're not a very nice person.

But if you're talking about building trust among peers and influential superiors, developing relationships, or schmoozing to gather important corporate intelligence, those don't seem like such heinous activities, do they?

So how does one become an able corporate politician? First, stop curling your lip into a sneer at the mere mention of it. Then, as always, do the research.

Before you join a company, find out about its political style by talking to current and former employees. Some places are more Machiavellian than others; will you be comfortable there?

David Hoffman, a former corporate sales executive and now a management consultant, says he didn't much like the politics he encountered. He says he once skipped a hastily called meeting of top executives to visit a major client. He was the only one invited who didn't make an appearance, and he was later told that he'd made a major career blunder.

Mr. Hoffman's aversion to office politics led him to abandon corporate life. It also led him to create the acidic computer game Suck Up, in which sycophantic middle managers vie for promotions by ingratiating themselves with senior management.

If you're politically averse, get small. Mr. Hoffman shrank his workaday universe to one. Others have opted for smaller companies or smaller operations tucked within corporate giants. The bigger and more complex the system in which you're operating, the more complicated and diabolical the politics. Or, simply stated: The more egos, the more politics.

In smaller units, the degree of political activity is often determined by the makeup of the leader. At the small, tightly knit San Francisco unit Terry South managed for Showtime Networks, politics was minimized, he says. He let his staff set its own goals and mission every six months. Conflicts and crises were aired openly in meetings, reducing whispering behind people's backs and innuendo. "If you're so focused on something, there's less time to worry about what so-and-so is saying behind your back," Mr. South says.

At another company early in his career, Mr. South learned the wages of mean-spirited politics. He, too, was a political player then, he confesses. "I rose quickly and got ahead of myself," he says. "I was trying to get senior management and everybody else to like me, but in a highly competitive environment, you can't please everybody."

Indeed, when a new, control-oriented CEO took over, Mr. South was banished to a make-work post away from corporate headquarters. "I realized I can't have everything," he says.

To be a good politician, you have to build up your defense as well as your offense. And nothing foils a backstabbing, glory-hogging peer quicker than an unassailable base of allies throughout the company. People who will tell you if anything important is going on that you should know about, who will stand up for you even if you're not around. You build that base by making yourself available to people, helping people, and thus building their respect and allegiance.

If you find yourself the target of backstabbing rivals and rumor-mongers, confront the miscreants. Make sure they learn the facts and calmly try to convince them to cease and desist. Ignoring the situation allows it to spread unchecked.

Beyond that, keep your boss and your network informed about what you've heard and what the truth is. If you've developed good allies, they will serve as a line of defense against lies and innuendo.

Finally, heaven help the poor soul who thinks he's above the fray, immune to office politics. Nobody is immune to it, and to think otherwise is to put yourself at risk.

Politics is an inevitable part of large organizations, but it needn't be nasty. The best political players build alliances based on trust, give-and-take, and open communication.

38

GETTING NOTICED
WITHOUT GETTING PUSHY

It's the eternal conundrum: How do I get recognized for my good work without becoming a self-aggrandizing climber? Is it enough simply to do good work? Can I trust the powers-that-be to notice?

The answer, I'm afraid, is no, you can't count on the attentiveness of your superiors. It could happen; the meritorious do sometimes triumph. Unfortunately, that isn't always the case.

There are ways to get the recognition you deserve. I'm not advocating hiring a personal PR person, although I know some who have. But there are more subtle ways of exposing your halogen-like brilliance to a wider population. Periodic project updates to the boss can help. But delete the I's from your writing and focus on the accomplishments of the team; if they succeed, you'll succeed. Also, resist the temptation to e-mail your report to every executive in the organization. Most could not care less and will probably be annoyed by your effrontery.

Alan Schonberg, president of Management Recruiters International, an executive recruiting firm, and author of *169 Ways to Score Points with Your Boss,* recalls one of his managers who fell into the self-promotion trap. He tried so vociferously to convince a group of executives to put him in charge of a new project that he eventually turned everyone against him. "He kept going on about how great he was and the wonderful things he was doing," Mr. Schonberg says. "It was a monologue, and it quickly became boring."

Longtime marketing executive Bob Wilson, of Evanston, Illinois, gained recognition internally by positioning himself as an external industry expert. That meant making himself available to reporters as an industry commentator, speaking at industry forums, and penning learned articles for industry publications. He was a frequent joiner of business and trade organizations, picking up committee chairmanships that marked him as an industry spokesperson.

And don't forget those humble in-house publications. Careerwise, that's targeted marketing, putting your message and expertise in front of the only audience that matters, eventually: your colleagues and superiors.

Another tried-and-true way to gain recognition is to make your boss look good. Taking on assignments that ease her load will earn you gratitude and recognition. So will bringing the manager new ideas that polish his résumé while providing new project teams for you to lead.

Of course nothing creates success like success. Amid all this positioning, don't forget to excel at what you do. Bob Skolnick rose to executive vice president of BAI Global, a market research firm in Tarrytown, New York, by developing and riding a hot product (a credit card tracking system). "It allowed me to develop expertise and gain credibility," he says. "That led to a larger leadership role."

The success of the product made Mr. Skolnick an expert everybody in the company wanted to talk to. And that, after all, is the best way to get recognition for yourself, by creating an internal buzz about your work.

All the self-promotion in the world can't overcome a lack of success, but a little subtle promotion can give a success story a winning edge.

39

LEARN TO NEGOTIATE; YOUR CAREER DEPENDS ON IT

It's something you do every day of your life, but may not realize it. And it's absolutely critical to career success.

I'm talking about negotiating. You may think that this is a skill valuable primarily to people putting together big mergers or hammering out labor contracts. You'd be wrong.

Have you and your spouse figured out who does which chores around the house? You're a negotiator.

Have you ever purchased a car or a house? You're a negotiator.

Got kids? Believe me, you're a negotiator.

At the negotiating tactics seminars given by Frank L. Acuff, author of *How to Negotiate Anything with Anyone, Anywhere Around the World,* attendees included managers from all over the corporate map—sales, materials, information systems, and human resources, among others.

With the growth of teams and project management, where lines of authority become blurry, the need to negotiate becomes especially important. And gone are the days when employes blindly do anything the boss orders. If you want to manage successfully, you'd better have good reasons for what you're asking and you'd better be darned persuasive. Need more staff or budget from the higher-ups? They're not going to come marching into your office to lavish goodies on you.

You'll have to convince them. And you'd better be persuasive if you want that big raise this year.

For Susan Pravda, co–managing partner of the Boston law office of Epstein, Becker & Green, "negotiations start in the morning when I have to get my daughter to brush her teeth." Ms. Pravda knows something about negotiating: her specialty is mergers and financings.

So what makes a good negotiator? Must you spend hours in front of the mirror practicing a menacing, Sonny Liston stare to intimidate the other side? Must you take a course in advanced table pounding? Must you engineer daring bluffs?

Actually, it requires none of the above. What it does demand is meticulous preparation, a willingness to understand the other side's needs, and an ability to build rapport and trust.

What kind of negotiation is it? asks Peter J. Pestillo, executive vice president of corporate relations for Ford Motor Co. and one of the automobile industry's preeminent labor negotiators. If it's a onetime event, he explains, you can concentrate solely on achieving the desired result. But if there's an ongoing relationship involved, victory comes from making both sides feel satisfied. "Take only what you need, and don't try to make anybody look bad," he advises.

Ms. Pravda stresses putting the other side at ease. Thus, while some experts might encourage you to invite the other side to your home field, giving you the advantage of comfort, Ms. Pravda prefers away games. "If you want something from someone," she says, "it's easier when they're comfortable."

She tries to find out everything she can about the other side. In merger talks, for example, she focuses on the owner, asking why he is selling and whether there are children or a spouse pushing him. Then she studies his advisers and how much each influences him.

Schmoozing is a critical part of preparation. "Don't walk in and start going through your list," she says. "If they have a baby picture on the desk, it doesn't hurt to say, 'Oh, is that a new grandchild?'" (A word of caution here: Unless you know it's a grandchild, it might be wiser to say something generic like "What a beautiful child" and let the owner fill in the blanks. What with the growth in second families and late starts in child rearing, you never know.)

Still, Ms. Pravda's point about personalizing the talks is well taken.

"People like to talk about themselves," she says. "It can segue into what you're trying to achieve."

Mr. Pestillo, known for arranging golf dates with union negotiators, is a master schmoozer. "If you know someone, you know some things that might be more important to him than to you," he says.

The toughest part of negotiating is listening—really listening—to the other side. "Most people who negotiate like to talk," Ms. Pravda explains. "But if you understand their problem, you can craft a creative solution. It doesn't hurt to say, 'I hear your problem; I don't know yet how to get there, but let me think about it.'"

Victoria Ruttenburg, a Washington, D.C., lawyer and mediator, recommends actually playing the role of the other side in practice sessions prior to the real thing. "Not just what position they're going to come up with, but why," she says. "And not just the business reason why, but what else is driving them."

Another crucial point: Before making your pitch, try to line up some allies. Ms. Ruttenburg recalls an inexperienced associate who requested a new assignment. Before doing so, however, he anticipated concerns about his experience and convinced a senior associate to volunteer as his supervisor. "So he'd already taken care of my concerns," Ms. Ruttenberg says.

Knowing when not to speak can be as important as knowing when to speak. When a young professional who had been fired decided he would be willing to take a $2,000 pay cut on his next job, executive coach Lewis Kravitz convinced him to keep that to himself until the prospective employer made the first move. Lo and behold, the candidate was offered $2,000 *above* his previous salary, leaving him stunned into momentary silence. Nature abhors a vacuum. Interpreting the silence incorrectly as disapproval, the interviewer promptly heaped another $2,000 onto his offer.

In this case, silence truly was golden.

Listening to the person across the table and understanding his or her priorities will get you more than talking about your needs.

40

LIVING WITH BAD BOSSES:
LOVE 'EM OR LEAVE 'EM

Bosses are the drivers of our careers—or the bane of our existence. They motivate us, shape our ideas, and lobby for us when promotions are on the line. Or they frustrate, infuriate, and even fire us. But whether we like them or not, they're always going to be there, and they will always possess inordinate power over our careers.

So you'd better be good at the care and feeding of bosses.

For instance, what if you're one of the unlucky souls whose boss is a real jerk. We've all been there at one time or another, stuck with a boss who is moody, tyrannical, uncommunicative, Machiavellian, or just plain incompetent.

Should you quit? What if you otherwise love your job, your pay, and your location? Should you let some first-class boor run you off? In the end, the answer may still be yes, but let's explore some other possibilities first.

Bad bosses come in all sorts of flavors, and your tolerance for those flavors will vary. There is the charismatic narcissist, who will find some way to blame every problem on you; the brute, who manages by terror; the paranoid, who infuses the department with the foreboding of doom that drives his life; the wimp, who hides from his staff in a closed office; the bureaucrat, who never met a foot-thick policy manual he didn't love; or his polar opposite, the crazy person, whose reckless, rule-bending management style may lead you to either a glorious result or a gory crack-up. There's also the manager I call "the Love Bug," a new age boss who is so busy nurturing and encouraging you that he neglects to mention that you're about to be fired; and the obsessive-compulsive, who seeks perfection and works until *you* drop.

Shailendra Gupta worked for a brilliant technician at a consulting firm. But brilliance often breeds arrogance. With this manager, Mr. Gupta recalls, you could never win an argument. His control extended to paper clips—he preferred square ones—and the commonplace oval ones were verboten.

To manage this disagreeable boss, Mr. Gupta recruited other managers who were in the boss's good graces to pitch proposals. When the boss objected to a potential new hire the staff liked, he and other managers used reverse psychology, saying they now agreed with the boss. "It wasn't two seconds before he flipped and said to hire the guy," recalls Mr. Gupta, now a consultant with Ernst & Young.

But tricks will get you only so far. In retrospect, Mr. Gupta feels he should have suppressed his ego, avoided confrontations, and worked harder to befriend the man outside the office. "I was one of those people who'd say, 'Why doesn't he understand?'" Mr. Gupta says. "Maybe my role should have been to coach him so he could understand."

The former chief financial officer of a manufacturing company says he worked for a boss who was such a penny-pincher that he routinely fired people just before their bonuses came due. He also charges that the boss pressured subordinates to fudge financial figures.

The former executive says he quickly learned the importance of developing allies throughout the company. "I'd work on the side with guys in other departments so we'd all have our act together" when we pitched him a plan, he says. Even if it doesn't always work, the company of fellow sufferers provides stress-relieving solace.

The executive also learned to fight another day. Instead of engaging in life-and-death struggles, he would often back off on an issue, file it away, and revive it a few months later after gathering more supporting data.

In the end, of course, the boss is still the boss, and you must learn to live with his or her quirks and vicissitudes. The best defense, always, is to make the boss look so good by your performance that he or she will be forced to leave you be. But sometimes, despite your best efforts, that just isn't enough. Sometimes the boss is so abusive, or so unethical, or so credit stealing, that you have to get out. As an advertising manager for a consumer products manufacturer, Dick Rosen worked under a boss who constantly second-guessed and bullied his staff. Mr. Rosen recalls a nasty incident over an alleged grammatical error in some ad copy. When proved wrong, the boss didn't even apologize. "You had to do it his way or it wasn't correct," Mr. Rosen says.

The mistake Mr. Rosen made was lingering for five years. He says he felt like "a battered wife," and like a battered wife, he stayed too long, hoping things would change. He survived that long by anticipating his boss's inevitable objections, even if it meant wasting time on irrelevant issues. He finally found contentment as a divisional vice president at Spiegel, the catalog company, which he later left after several years. He then ran the package division of Ambrosi & Associates, a retail and catalog advertising company in Chicago.

Sometimes, though, having a bad boss isn't such a bad deal. Lisa Grace was the head teller for a bank branch whose technically oriented manager was sadly miscast. "He didn't know the business and didn't want to take time to learn it," she says. "He spent most of his time rewiring the building."

As a result, Ms. Grace and a friend who managed customer service got to run the bank, make his sales calls, and attend training seminars he shunned.

"He seldom questioned anything," says Ms. Grace, now a mortgage broker in Fort Myers, Florida. There were times the women wished he would carry his weight, but, Ms. Grace says, nonmanagers are better than micromanagers. "You just have to work around them," she says. "You can have the opportunity to do their job and learn a great deal and prepare yourself for a better position."

Try managing a bad boss by building alliances with co-workers, anticipating objections, or making the boss look good, but don't overdo it. Sometimes it's simply better to leave than try to cope with an abusive boss.

41

SURVIVING A NEW BOSS

Breaking in a new boss is one of the truly unsettling moments in anyone's career. Having just gotten used to that neurotic, fidgety last boss, you're now suddenly starting over with someone who doesn't know you, the operation, or, in the worst-case scenario, squat.

But that lack of knowledge may be your best asset. Who will provide this new superior with the critical knowledge he or she needs to succeed? If you're smart, it will be you.

When Hibernia Bank got a new CEO in 1983, J. Thomas Van Berkem, senior vice president of human resources, was the sole senior executive to survive the subsequent purge. He did it, he says, by becoming a fount of information that his new boss needed: the viability of the business plan, the pros and cons of the executive team.

"If you find ways to make people successful, that will be remembered," says Mr. Van Berkem, senior vice president of human resources at Wellpoint Health Networks, a Thousand Oaks, California, health insurance holding company.

First impressions are critical. New bosses want to know if you're open to change and eager to be on the new team. At your first meeting, listen a lot, Mr. Van Berkem advises. "Don't go in with your own canned agenda; come across as competent and confident without being pushy or presumptuous."

You can also gather some information on your own. Quiz your new boss's former colleagues on his idiosyncrasies. Does he use military analogies in his speech? "If that's the case, you might want to avoid symphony analogies," says Robin Klein, a senior vice president at Chase Manhattan Bank, who has considerable experience with management changes.

What are the new person's hot buttons? What should you avoid? "You want to hear stories of when things didn't work out," she says.

Mr. Van Berkem recalls how such knowledge helped one department head at a previous employer adapt to a new boss. "She told you the history of Wall Street before you could get a position out of her," he recalls. But the new boss was a "you've got thirty seconds to make your point" guy, he says. Thanks to the scouting report and some coaching, the wordy department head survived.

Your company's human resources department might also help. Some HR departments work up detailed personality profiles of new executives as part of what they call an "insertion process." The idea is to give new and old knowledge that will help them coexist and avoid costly executive flameouts.

But make no mistake: This is a dangerous moment in your career. So many new bosses come in with the idea that they must wield a heavy broom to justify their new position. Or they simply feel more comfortable surrounding themselves with people with whom they've worked before. Carving a niche for yourself in this environment isn't just about avoiding a critical faux pas or not being too pushy. Eventually you must show that you can contribute—indeed, that you're damn near indispensable. You can use the knowledge of the organization that you have and that the boss doesn't to offer a different point of view. Your intricate knowledge of how the company works is your edge. "You're showing you have the confidence to bring in other information that might be helpful," Ms. Klein says.

This can be tricky business. You want to speak your mind but not be seen as resisting the new regime. New bosses are hypersensitive to resistance. So don't just recycle old ideas or dig in your heels with an "if it ain't broke don't fix it" attitude. You want to show that while you might have differences, when a decision is made, "you're committed to new management's point of view and making it happen," she adds.

Of course, there's only so far you can bend, and if you truly believe that your philosophy or style is wildly incompatible with the new regime's, it's best to look for signs of that early and bow out before you're booted out. Trying to force a square peg into a round hole can be costly, leading to disaffection and bitterness or turning you into a corporate chameleon without strong convictions of your own. Either one is a career killer.

Dick Sethi survived a host of executive changes in his years as assistant director of executive education at AT&T. Mastering that sudden shift in the political winds has become as important to career success as results, he says.

Mr. Sethi, now director of executive leadership programs for Thomson Corp., also sees this as the perfect time for some self-assessment. The changes at AT&T forced him to reevaluate his strengths and weaknesses and the quality of his relationships with colleagues.

He decided he was too abrupt with people, interrupting them too frequently in conversations. He found he learned more, and offended less, by listening more. "If you have a new boss, you have a great opportunity to figure out who you are," he says. "How you conduct yourself makes all the difference."

A *new boss who doesn't know you is looking for your support, not your agenda.*

42

GOING OVER THE BOSS'S HEAD

Want to play Russian roulette with your career? Try going over your boss's head when you don't like his or her decision.

Few issues in corporate life raise such deep concerns about loyalty, betrayal, and ethics. Opinions on this touchy subject range from "never, ever, ever," as one executive coach put it, to "if you don't, you're not doing your job," in the words of a corporate training consultant. In between, there are enough gray areas to paint an elephant.

In general, I lean toward the "no way, nohow" school. Part of my reluctance in this matter comes from personal experience. Early in my career, when my boss rejected a story idea I was excited about, I went over his head to another editor, who approved the idea. I'll never forget the look of anger and betrayal on my boss's face when I smugly informed him of my end-around. I felt like a cad. He was a good boss, an excellent mentor, and didn't deserve that kind of treatment. To me, no story was worth risking that relationship, and I dropped the idea on the spot. It wasn't even a close call.

At most companies, this attitude is ingrained. At a workshop for the managers of a major retail distributor, corporate trainer Jon Spera urges them to push their ideas for change more aggressively, even if their bosses object. "Why don't you go over his head?" he prods a manager who complained of an obstructionist superior. Several managers chuckled and said that wasn't the way things were done in their organization. "How would you feel if someone under you went over your head?" one manager asked. Another told of the time he complained about his boss to his boss's boss, who promptly reported the conversation, "line for line," to the bypassed manager. "Until he decided to leave, he made my life miserable," the manager said.

Nevertheless, as the years whiz by, I realize there are situations—extreme ones, mind you—where bypassing the boss is unavoidable. And even in those cases, your approach must be taken with the utmost sensitivity and diplomacy.

One woman worked for a volatile boss who often humiliated subordinates in front of others. Most of the people who worked for him ended up quitting or being fired, she recalls. After a meeting in which she thought she had performed well, he angrily vowed to cut off her access to other decision makers. Years later, she still doesn't want herself or the company identified.

What really grated was that he wouldn't tell her what she was doing wrong; so she decided to solicit the views of other executives at the company. She knew it could cost her her job but figured she probably would be fired before long anyway. What did she have to lose? "It's not such a bad thing to say, 'I'm unhappy, I have to do something,'" she says.

Wisely, though, she didn't use those meetings to plead for relief or whine about her tyrant boss. "I said, 'Tell me what I can do to better serve you,'" she says—and then listened. One executive told her she should have been promoted long ago. Another helped her make contacts that led to a career as a consultant.

Unfortunately, more companies than not still view the act as insubordination. And once you get that label, you risk losing the trust of future bosses. And higher-ups may offer little solace; don't forget that this is probably someone they appointed to his current job. They won't like being told they've made a mistake in judgment.

So one measure for making this difficult decision should be: Is this issue worth the risk and the bad feelings? Only if the decision would put the company into fiscal, ethical, or legal jeopardy. It would have to be an issue that would prompt you to leave if it wasn't corrected.

In those circumstances, I'd still give the boss a chance to make things right first. Maybe you're reading the situation wrong and there's a good explanation for his behavior. Maybe you can work things out. If he still stonewalls you, say you feel it's important enough to discuss with higher-ups. Sneaking around will label you as untrustworthy.

In any case, you'd better be prepared to leave, under your own power or not. Start exploring other possibilities, both inside and outside the company. The woman who sidestepped her boss, knowing that her time there was probably short, started participating in outside groups and became a conference speaker to make contacts.

Going over the boss's head is advisable only if you are suicidal or you're going to be dead meat anyway.

43

TEACHING AN OLD BOSS NEW TRICKS

Bill Prince is living proof that, while it isn't easy, a leopard can change his spots and a tyrant can be tamed.

Mr. Prince's fast-track managerial career at BellSouth was derailed by his coarse bedside manner. He bulldozed his way through problems, projects, and—when they got in his way—people. He was demeaning to subordinates and disdainful of bosses. "I went through life thinking I was a top manager and couldn't understand why I didn't become a vice president," he says. "As it turned out, I had some blind spots in my management style that I wasn't aware of."

But with the help of a wise and persistent boss and a program that forced him to face his deficiencies, Mr. Prince changed his style. That enabled him to start his own business with an eye toward expansion, something he would never have risked before for fear of alienating his staff.

Mr. Prince is illustrative of a generation of American managers who grew up with the belief that fear motivates and that leadership meant "my way or the highway." But in the information age, products increasingly come not from an assembly line, but from employees' heads. And with job-hopping now more common, managers are finding that showing a more compassionate side is a better way to retain talent and to motivate.

When Mr. Prince joined BellSouth in 1964 after graduating from college, the only thing that seemed to matter for managers was getting results. After fifteen years, he had become a middle manager and part of the company's high-potential development program by turning around underperforming organizations in a dozen cities. But he says he did it in a "brusque and unfeeling manner," firing people in droves. And those he sacked may have been the lucky ones: survivors were treated coldly, praised infrequently, and publicly demeaned for mistakes. Eventually, Mr. Prince's career bogged down. Others got promotions he felt he deserved, and he grew bitter toward higher management. "I didn't always treat them with the respect I should have," he says.

When a general manager didn't fire an employee for a security violation, as he had recommended, for example, Mr. Prince went over his head to suggest disciplinary measures—for the general manager. "I had low tolerance for executives who wouldn't deal with summary judgment when I felt we needed it," he says. After thirty years with the company, Mr. Prince found himself in an executive support position, headed nowhere. So he quit in 1994 and joined A&A Services, a telecommunications services outsourcing firm owned by Art Hall, a former BellSouth colleague. He started as a senior consultant and was named executive director within ninety days. But Mr. Prince's tough-guy management style hadn't changed. Mr. Hall recalls driving home from a seminar and asking if Mr. Prince would be able to respect him as boss. His cold response: "That's up to you," according to Mr. Hall.

Mr. Prince acknowledges he didn't show Mr. Hall the proper respect. "It was like, 'Just get out of my way and I'll get the sales and profits,'" he says. Employees complained that he pushed too hard and treated them rudely, Mr. Hall recalls. "People were saying, 'This guy is toxic.'" So Mr. Hall called Mr. Prince in for a talk, offering to find him a program that would help him change his behavior. Mr. Prince got the message: "If I didn't want the help, he'd arrange a graceful exit."

The cure was an intensive leadership development program run by

Atlanta psychologist Robert L. Turknett. He put the tyrannical exec through a battery of tests and sought assessments from twenty-two former bosses, peers, and subordinates going back fifteen years. "He had a bull-in-a-china-shop approach to managing people," Mr. Turknett concluded.

Mr. Prince learned that people saw him as overly frank and often offensive. Nonverbal signals were also a problem. "I could look at you and you would know you were an inch tall," he says. He traced some of this behavior to a broken home. "It instilled in me a hard-nosed disposition," he says. "I was going to do whatever it took to survive."

Fortunately, he was also a man of strong will. He started making a list of desired behaviors:

- **Treat employees the same as clients.**
- **Don't go home with any relationships still damaged.**
- **Take responsibility for your own actions.** "I always said, 'That's just the way I am,'" he says. "Bob told me that being hard-nosed was a choice."

Mr. Turknett gave him homework: Focus on one person for a week, stressing the positive things that person has done. Write the things you value about the person. "He would come back and say, 'It's like a miracle; he's like my best buddy—he'll do anything for me,'" Mr. Turknett recalls.

Now, as the CEO of his own company, Mr. Prince is careful to focus on fixing the problem, not condemning the person who made the mistake. "Ten years ago, I probably would have glared at that person, gritted my teeth to indicate how upset I was with him personally," he says. "And I would have done it in front of other people." Mr. Hall confirms that the change in Mr. Prince's approach was dramatic. "When I asked him, 'Where do you want to go to lunch?' he said, 'Where do you want to go, Art?'" Mr. Hall says. "Before that, no matter what, he wanted to make the decision."

Managers should manage with compassion and care if they want to retain and motivate the talent they need. Sooner or later, most managers from the brutish school of management find their careers stalled.

PART SEVEN

ALTERNATE PATHS TO GLORY

44

THE PERILS AND PROMISE OF
TURNING YOUR HOBBY
INTO A CAREER

When I first met Steve Sansweet, he seemed like a fairly level-headed, normal guy. Little did I know.

At the time (the mid-1970s), we were both reporters in the *Wall Street Journal*'s Los Angeles bureau, a noble and relatively mainstream career path. Both of us would go on to become bureau chiefs with the paper. But Steve was leading a double life: he had a hobby, although that's a bit like calling Mt. Everest a nice little hill.

On two acres in rural Petaluma, California, Mr. Sansweet's modest, ranch-style home is dwarfed by the adjacent, five-thousand-square-foot barn in which resides his collection of toys and memorabilia related to George Lucas's Star Wars movies. In a space that could handle a small convention, model spaceships dangle from the ceiling above an imposing array of toys, video games, posters, movies, boxes upon boxes of knickknacks, life-size mannequins of Yoda, Darth Vader, and Jar Jar Binks, and much, much more. It is, he claims, the largest private Star Wars collection in existence—so large, he has never been able to summon the time or energy to completely catalog it or estimate its worth.

As Mr. Sansweet's avocation grew like Jabba the Hut, it eventually subsumed his journalistic career. Today, besides the considerable job of managing his collection, he is the director of content management for Lucasfilm, Mr. Lucas's production company.

How many of you have dreamed about making a career of your sideline passion, whether it's an art collector who wants to operate a gallery or a Hot Wheels or Barbie aficionado who wants to work for Mattel, or a golf nut who longs to own a pro shop or a land a cushy job with Callaway or Ping? Remember the bank executive, mentioned earlier, who quit to buy and sell toy soldiers, a lifelong obsession?

It's an alluring idea, since it marries your career with your true love. Isn't that what everybody supposedly craves? And generally, it means swerving out of the corporate fast lane, an idea with much curb appeal in these days of rampaging entrepreneurism and anticorporate sentiments. What could be better?

But always remember (as the song goes): "When your heart's on fire, smoke gets in your eyes." Certainly, some hobbies can be developed into parallel careers and provide backup revenue in case your primary career falters. But this isn't the road to glory for most people. So before walking blithely into chaos, think carefully about the answers to these key questions: Does a legitimate, profit-making niche exist in this field? If you're giving up your day job to trade Pokémon cards on eBay, it's time for a reality check and, perhaps, commitment to the nearest mental health facility. If there is a living to be made, can you pursue it in an objective and businesslike manner? Think about it. How many times has your fervor for your hobby overwhelmed sweet reason and common sense? It's hard to be bottom line oriented about your true love.

Finally, do you have the needed skills for this career byroad? If you're going solo, are you a self-starter, an avid and knowledgeable marketer and salesperson? If a corporate job is involved, do you have the qualifications for the jobs available? Lucasfilm is constantly besieged by starry-eyed dreamers who want to hitch a ride on the Millennium Falcon of careers but have little concept of what this path requires and what they have to contribute. The company took on Mr. Sansweet, but not without considerable hesitation. And it did so only because his writing ability, his contacts in the Star Wars toy and fan worlds, and his extensive knowledge of the business world had tangible economic value.

For Mr. Sansweet, the career switch has been satisfying, albeit diffi-cult and not without some sacrifice. How did he alter his career direction? A boyhood fascination with science fiction was reawak-ened by a story he did on toy collecting, and the 1977 release of *Star Wars* sank the hook in deeper. When a colleague (not me, thankfully) threw away a promotional brochure for the soon-to-be-released movie, Mr. Sansweet fished it out of the trash. The brochure is now worth about $150, he estimates. By the time *The Empire Strikes Back* was released in 1980, Star Wars collecting was a "full-blown obses-sion," he says.

For the next two decades, he juggled his double life. He became Los Angeles bureau chief in 1987, while traveling far and wide to attend fan conventions and research the books he began to write about the Star Wars phenomenon in his spare time. He became a reg-ular commentator on QVC shopping shows as a Star Wars merchan-dise expert. These sidelines provided an income cushion—at least the funds he didn't sink into even more purchases.

As the hobby grew, though, so did the potential for conflict, although he says he was careful to keep his two lives separate. While he made sure he wasn't identified as a *Wall Street Journal* employee on QVC, the newspaper's editors grew uneasy about having the bureau chief who supervised entertainment industry coverage appearing as a pitchman for objets d'entertainment. "Toward the end I was getting signals that my appearances on the QVC shows were a bone of con-tention," he recalls.

By the mid-1990s, the stress of maintaining his dual careers was getting difficult to bear. Mired in what was supposed to be a short-term *Star Wars Encyclopedia* project that had swollen to three years while heading into his ninth year as a bureau chief—well past the average tenure for that job—he needed a change. Passing on *Journal* jobs he describes as "substantial," he focused on Lucasfilm. "When George announced he was going to do the next three episodes and would redo the first three, I thought, If there was ever a time to make a career change, this is it," Mr. Sansweet says. "I couldn't think of any-thing I'd rather do or any place I'd rather be than inside Lucasfilm when George Lucas was making three new Star Wars movies. This has defined me so much for so long in my life."

But Lucasfilm couldn't figure out what to do with him initially, he says. "Because I came from outside, I think some people at Lucasfilm were a little leery of me," Mr. Sansweet says. "They thought I was a Johnny-one-note, 'the toy guy,' who knew something about collectibles but wasn't interested in the films." This isn't true, he says. "My passion comes from the films."

He persisted, and when Lucasfilm needed someone who could explain to disgruntled fans why the studio was redoing the original three films, they thought of Steve and his extensive contacts with fan organizations. He convinced the filmmaker to renegotiate his contract on the encyclopedia, because of the extra time needed for the project, and add in part-time work as fan liaison. The company said it would try to find something more permanent. It was a significant career risk, including a noticeable cut in pay. But, he adds, "it was a risk I was willing to take."

In any such situation, a career change of this magnitude is a considerable risk. But Mr. Sansweet had picked the right time for such a move—when his financial cushion was substantial and when Lucasfilm was gearing up for a big new marketing push. As in almost anything, good timing can reduce risk considerably.

Still, he needed a plan. Once the Lucasfilm people got to know him better, he hoped, he would be able to craft a job that would play to his strengths. To reach that point, though, he had to get closer to the company's beating heart in Northern California. Commuting all the way from Los Angeles to a company that thrived on creativity and constant brainstorming kept him an outsider. There was always the Friday meeting he had to skip to catch his plane or the late arrivals on Monday morning. It wasn't until he moved to Petaluma, close to Lucasfilm's headquarters, that he "felt on solid ground," he says.

Proximity paid off when he and the company crafted his current full-time position, which he describes as being the gatekeeper of Star Wars still images. He decides who gets to use the 50,000 or more stills from each movie and when. It involves licensing, publishing, websites, and fan magazines. In addition, he still organizes fan conventions and serves, he says, as "the father confessor for fan groups around the world."

It hasn't been a joyride of unrelenting fun. "This isn't the fantasy land everyone expects," he says. "It involves hard work, high expectations, and considerable stress." Prior to the release of *The Phantom Menace* in 1999, he says, Lucasfilm employees worked incredibly long hours. "There's a lot of stress," he says. "A lot of people left after the movie was released."

Still, there are those magical days that remind him why he persisted. He recalls walking over to the licensing department one day, where a colleague pulled out some new toys from Japan he hadn't known about. "We took them out and played with them on the floor, and it was really cool," he says, grinning broadly. "I can still get excited by that."

Remember the old Beatles song "All You Need Is Love?" It isn't true. You also need the right skills, personality, and emotional makeup to make a career out of your hobby.

45

ALTERNATIVE WORK ARRANGEMENTS: BEATING THE ODDS AND MAKING THEM WORK

The most overhyped concept of the 1990s? A great candidate, outside of the Internet, of course, is alternative work arrangements. Flexible work proselytizers predicted an explosion of part-time, job-sharing, and telecommuting arrangements to accommodate all those folks out there yearning for a balance between work and family.

Somehow, it just didn't take.

To be sure, the population of flex workers has increased, but it remains a blip on the screen. Why? Management has resisted, fearful that workers just wouldn't be efficient if they weren't chained to their desks each day. That may be why telecommuting has been such a tough sell. Keeping the lines of communication wide open, coordinating work assignments and team projects, and assuring accountability for performance goals have made telecommuting the most difficult of the flextime concepts.

That was predictable. Not so predictable was resistance from workers, who either feared their career momentum would stall or simply craved the social interaction of the workplace.

Besides, how many roses can you smell in one lifetime?

Still, the concept remains a seductive one for those who place family ahead of ambition or have special circumstances that, at least temporarily, force them to slow down the career train—young children or ailing parents, for example. And yes, the majority of those pursuing these arrangements are still women. But let's face reality: Putting yourself on a flexible work schedule isn't likely to enhance your bid for corporate stardom. Some managers will inevitably consider you a bothersome creature who isn't "committed" to the company or your career. So the real goal here is to do it in a way that inflicts little or no damage to your career and may even get you an "attagirl" for soldiering on bravely.

For those trying to sell the boss on some kind of flexible arrangement, remember the doctor's maxim: First, do no harm. Make sure that the arrangement won't disrupt your department's schedule or efficiency and that you, personally, remain at least as productive as you were before. Second, anticipate management's concerns and resolve them before they're even raised. Volunteer to train anyone picking up any of your former duties, for example. Draw up a proposal—complete with performance goals—that meets both your needs and the company's and lays out specifically how work will be done. (Make sure it's realistic, or you may find yourself putting in full-time hours for part-time pay.)

An exemplar of this portion of the workforce is Rosemary Mans, who, when I first met her, was a vice president of flexibility programs for the Bank of America in San Francisco—and worked part-time. She wanted to change people's perceptions of flexible work schedules. She saw them not as lifestyle accommodations, but as another way of thinking about how to get work done. "If we can help people, fine, but you don't give away the store to be nice," she said.

Ms. Mans's philosophy of flexibility is simple: "Look for work that needs to be done, shape it, and sell it," she explains.

Which is precisely what she did. In 1988, having just completed a grueling three-year project on public-private partnerships for child care for the Bank of America Foundation, Ms. Mans wanted to push further into work and family issues. She also wanted to get more balance in her own life. So she proposed a solution—a part-time position as manager of work-family programs—and then sold the heck out of it to corporate management until they buckled. Then, in 1993, after a year of pitching the idea to various management types, she convinced the bank to create her current job, which gave her an even broader mandate.

At times, she admitted, her part-time job has been anything but. Still, she said she felt less stress, discovered off-the-job ways to express her creativity, and felt "more connected" with family. She also contended that she was more focused and productive at work and that her case wasn't an exception.

She wrote and distributed guidebooks for employees, always pushing the idea that flexibility can be a smart way to reengineer work. Chapters included "Are There Business Benefits?" and "Does It Make Sense?" She cited experiments where branch banks were able to stay open longer because of flexible scheduling. Also, she noted, flexible arrangements can reduce the cost of office space, expand access to equipment, and cut payroll expense.

Another experiment that has popped up in recent years is job sharing for managers. Now that's a tough one, since you not only have to parcel out hours and chores, you have to handle dual temperaments and egos, the dangers of mixed messages to the troops, and the fear that important issues will fall through the cracks. How are decisions made? How are disagreements resolved? Who gets to pick the office decor?

Carrie Majeske and Nancy Cragel have served as co-managers of corporate products requirements planning for Ford Motor Co. for four years, starting when Nancy became pregnant for the first time. "One of the challenges," Ms. Majeske says, "is trying to get into each other's heads."

Even though they didn't know each other prior to playing sharesies at work, the two say they have similar attitudes and strategic thinking patterns. "Sometimes we finish each other's sentences," says Ms. Majeske.

Still, job sharing always seems a bit awkward to me. In this case, both managers work on Monday, then split the rest of the week. They hand off the management ball through copious notes and hallway conversations. At meetings, they take extra notes to make sure the other understands what happened. They will talk on the phone for an hour to resolve a disagreement but say they can't ever remember becoming angry. Ms. Cragel credits their success in part to their noncompetitive natures. "You're not competing for face time or credit; when you present something, it's from both of you."

While this two-headed managerial monster hardly seems the most efficient of models, Ms. Cragel notes the upside: "Things don't drop off the table because you haven't written them down," she says.

There's also that "two heads are better than one" thing. Because they came from different parts of the company, they occasionally fill in each other's blank spots. Ms. Majeske recalls a discussion of environmental issues where she focused almost exclusively on the requirements of government entities; Ms. Cragel pointed out the need to think more about nongovernmental organizations and their concerns. Ms. Majeske hadn't even thought of that.

They've done enough of that to work through four positions of increasing responsibility together. Still, they're not sure how long they'll continue on this path. Even if they part, they feel they'll be better managers for the experience. "During the day, sometimes I think, How would Carrie attack this problem?" Ms. Cragel says. "It's challenging us to grow."

In the end, she believes, "it's a wash between the inefficiency and the 'two heads are better than one' thing."

So what's the key to making these arrangements work? Plan ahead to minimize any disruptions in the workplace. Make your manager your best friend. Converse frequently in person or by phone, fax, or e-mail about what you're doing and the progress you're making. This will make him or her more comfortable with a lower level of monitoring and control. Stay abreast of developments. It's easy for flextimers to get left behind as priorities and projects shift. Be creative. Just because you're telecommuting or working part-time doesn't mean you can't identify and solve key problems or volunteer for important projects. Make sure that home and family commitments aren't so great that you can't adjust your schedule to help out in an emergency.

To some extent, you must demonstrate that even if you're not there all the time, your commitment to the job is just as great, if not greater.

Careful structuring of an alternative work arrangement to show how it helps your company as much as it helps you can overcome the inherent bias against such arrangements.

46

LIVING LIFE AS A PILOT FISH

There is more than one way to skin the career cat. Are you tired of corporate life, with all its bureaucracy, politics, and crazy bosses, but not quite ready to go it alone as a consultant or full-fledged entrepreneur?

Consider the pilot fish, a small marine creature who survives by hanging around large marine creatures and living off their leavings.

The human equivalent is exemplified by James McGowan, Mark Dresner, and Drew Arlo. In 1994, the trio of former Digital Equipment salesmen bought a controlling interest in Infinite Technology Group, Mineola, New York, as a way to escape the then uncertain environment of corporate life. But they minimized the risk of this entrepreneurial venture by swimming alongside their former employer, so to speak. They identified niche services that weren't economical for a giant company like Digital to continue to provide to its customers, but were just right for a little pilot fish, and then contracted—with Digital's blessing and marketing support—to provide those services, which represent the bulk of Infinite Technology's revenues.

As more companies sell off nonessential businesses or outsource services, there are growing opportunities to create pilot fish companies. It's an excellent way for corporate managers and professionals to exercise their entrepreneurial muscles by utilizing existing expertise and business connections. Examples range from a departing manager continuing to provide his or her services to the company as an outside contractor to companies that spin off entire departments to employee-owned operations.

When properly structured, the arrangement works well for all concerned. The pilot fish starts life with a relatively secure revenue stream. The customer gets more personalized service. And the big fish dumps profit-draining fringe operations while still keeping customers serviced and happy. "They know the customer base," says Bill Watts, Digital's New York State sales manager, of the Infinite trio. "They know the end users and the markets they're trying to get into."

One marketing edge for Infinite, Mr. Dresner notes, is the comfort level Digital managers have in recommending the company, because they know the principals and their capabilities intimately. He says Digital's salespeople often call them to pitch an account jointly. "They know our ability to close big sales," he says.

Mr. Dresner says he and his partners probably could have stayed at Digital indefinitely, but they had become conscientious objectors in the seemingly endless restructuring wars that were common in the early 1990s. Mr. McGowan had gone through workforce reductions at AT&T, Xerox, and Digital. Mr. Dresner was making more than $120,000 a year selling to big accounts but realized that his chances of becoming a manager weren't good. Mr. Arlo faced a choice of moving laterally or leaving. "I couldn't deal with the fact that someone else was deciding my future," he says, "so I opted out."

The first step to life as a successful pilot fish is identifying a potentially profitable niche that your current employer isn't providing or that you can provide more efficiently. From his perspective as a recruiter of outside software providers, Mr. McGowan was able to catalog areas of customer need that Digital wasn't offering. For example, Infinite provided customized computer maintenance service to a bank that bought 5,000 Digital computers—one-on-one service that would have been time-consuming and unprofitable for the larger company. Infinite generated millions in revenue by providing a service—recycling used computer equipment—long ignored by Digital's sales force.

Mr. McGowan, who had been plotting his corporate escape for years, realized early on that his internal relationships were just as crucial as, if not more so than, his contacts outside the company. "If you keep your network intact, you can capitalize on people at the company and people who have left the company," he says. He constructed a chart of Digital people with whom he needed to connect, as well as the people who advised them. "You have to identify the weaknesses in your network and work on that," he says.

To that end, Mr. McGowan says he has even backed away from potential sales to help his Digital contacts improve their positions within the company. "It's money out of your pocket," he says, "but the relationship is as important as the sale."

It's also important to remember that you're embarking on a journey to a strange land where you'll need to develop survivor skills. Mr. Dresner took some computer science classes to broaden his knowledge of the customer's needs. "It isn't enough to know how a piece of hardware works," he explains. "You have to understand all the ways the underlying technology can be used so you can develop creative solutions to customers' problems."

If you're a veteran salesman starting your own business, you should consider management courses as well. And don't fall into the trap of relying solely on your relationship with your former employer. It's a convenient way to get your company launched, but things can change too rapidly these days. The company could be bought by a rival, and the contacts you relied on could be sent packing. You could develop your niches so well, your former employer might decide they were viable markets after all and apply its considerable clout to reclaiming them.

So start developing independent sources of revenue to bulwark your company's financial standing and spread your risk. A pilot fish doesn't have to be monogamous.

The ability to spot a niche opportunity and to develop close relationships with co-workers can allow you to have a lucrative career outside of, but parallel to, your current employer.

47

WOMEN WHO BREAK THE MOLD

It's tough enough for a woman to crack the executive ranks at most companies. What if that company is still largely a boys club, in a business where women were traditionally shut out?

Susana Florian and Christine Davis became vice presidents in industries that were male dominated long after that ceased to be fashionable. Ms. Florian is a civil and structural engineer, Ms. Davis a software engineer. When they were starting out, female managers in those industries were indeed rare.

But these days, I believe, being a woman in a nontraditional role can be an advantage. Many companies in these fields are seeking out women aggressively, because it's the politically correct thing to do. And for the few who take that path, there is far less competition from other women.

BE&K, a Birmingham, Alabama, construction and engineering company, has promoted several of its veteran female employees to supervisory positions; that's still a rarity in the industry. Mike Goodrich, the CEO, says the company wants to bring women into management ranks at all levels.

Today, a woman in engineering or construction has "as good a chance for advancement as her male counterpart, maybe even better," he says.

When Ms. Florian came to the United States from Romania twenty years ago with a degree in civil and structural engineering, she was forced to start as a lower-level technician. She eventually rose to vice president of corporate marketing and quality for Michael Baker Corp., a Pittsburgh engineering and construction company.

Getting there wasn't easy. "I was tested on each new assignment by people assigned to me or working with me," she says. When problems arose, subordinates often wouldn't volunteer solutions. "They waited to see what I would say," she says.

She advises women to build up credibility through a variety of technical assignments before tackling management. "For the first eighteen years of my career, I advanced strictly in the technical area," she says. "I feel my recommendations have more weight because I've experienced the work."

To gain that credibility, she tackled difficult and risky assignments. But that also meant high visibility. She introduced the company to the total quality management concept, for example. That system, designed to continuously improve products, has foundered at other companies. She later headed a new corporate marketing department, a function that had previously been handled at the division level.

Ms. Davis, a young math whiz, envisioned a traditional female career as a teacher of mathematics. Then she discovered computers. That led her to Texas Instruments, the big Dallas semiconductor manufacturer, where she became vice president of engineering for the systems group. Like Ms. Florian, she pursued what she saw as the most difficult projects, such as creating an engineering organization that cut across divisional lines.

"In your first few years at a company, you have to get the tough jobs," she says, "and then you're seen as a leader."

Women need to be especially careful to avoid falling into administrative black holes. Ms. Davis volunteered for all kinds of software projects and kept asking for more responsibility.

"I kept coming up with ideas of how to improve things," she says. "The more you do, the more you get asked to do."

Her alliance with an elite group of technicians also helped. When their stars rose, so did hers. "You'd love to think this is a world where who you know doesn't count, but it does," she says. "People are afraid to promote people they don't know; you have to get exposure."

Most of all, you can't assume that the powers-that-be understand your ambitions or what's best for you in your career development. You have to continually speak up, letting them know. When you choose the road less traveled, she says, you must "have a vision of where you want to go and let the gatekeepers know where you want to go."

In other words, don't let the men make assumptions about you. They'll usually be wrong.

In a biased world, women aspiring to senior management must take extra steps to demonstrate their expertise in core areas or risk being pigeonholed.

48

LIVING LA VIDA FREE AGENCY

Okay, let's talk about this whole free agency thing.

It is, after all, one of those guru-concocted, sound-bite, made-for-dust-jacket phrases that drive me crazy. We have always had free agents; we just called them consultants, freelancers, or the unemployed.

On the other hand, there is something different about today's breed of free agent, and that difference can benefit your career.

In previous generations, free agency was largely involuntary, as in the countless legions of jobless who called themselves "consultants" when they were between gainful employment. But today's crowd has a totally different mind-set; they see it as a separate career path—one that leads to independence, a wide variety of career experiences, and control over their career movement. They are the children of the betrayed boomer generation, who saw their parents get cut adrift by the companies with whom they had spent most of their careers. While most operate independently and on a project-by-project basis, true free agency is a state of mind. If you have the right mind-set, you could be a vice president at General Electric and still consider yourself a free agent. To me, all that means is that you maintain your independence and sense of control over your career destiny, wherever you work.

Jerry Flach considers herself a free agent, even though she's a full-time manager with an investment management firm in New Jersey. That's because, she says, she is loyal first to her "value system" and doesn't get involved in corporate politics. If the infighting gets too nasty, or she feels she isn't adding value, or the company isn't utilizing her skills fully, she will leave. That's a free agent mentality. When she hit a glass ceiling at one job and was given a very narrow job, she jumped to another company that offered an opportunity to manage, with a mandate to effect change. "When I left that company after twelve years, I finally felt like a free agent," she says. "It was so exciting; I was putting systems in, and I was involved in so many things."

To be a free agent, she says, you must be "devoted to bettering yourself constantly and not having the fear of losing your job," she says. "I will never let fear paralyze me."

Many describe it as having a consultant mentality, whether or not you're on the payroll full-time. Theoretically, that allows you to speak freely and candidly to your boss because you're not invested in the status quo. You look at the organization as if you were an outsider, and because such candor is risky in companies that speak longingly of "buy-in" and "being in alignment," you are ready to leave at a moment's notice. Of course, I say theoretically, because most people can't reach that divine state. Whether you're on the payroll or working as an independent contractor, somebody is signing your check, and that makes it difficult to be completely candid.

One aspect of free agency that has gathered much attention is the growth of websites that serve as open marketplaces where companies can bid on talent for specific projects. Still, for those free agents who are winging it on their own, success, as with most things related to careers, will depend on the extent and quality of their contacts and their ability to market themselves successfully. And because in a free agent free-for-all you're never sure what skills will be needed or in demand, there's a constant drive to add arrows to your quiver of skills. To maintain your competitive edge, you can't stand still.

Free agency gurus will tell you that those skills and your marketing ability will separate the stars from the also-rans in this new economy field. Of course, we all know better, don't we? There is always a certain amount of politics and rear-end smooching that goes into building a successful free agent career, as it does with any other career path. It's all about building relationships. Any of today's generation who say they've been freed from office political wrangling is deep into self-delusion.

So don't be misguided. Listen to Marlin Pohlman, a technology consultant, talking about his interaction with clients: "No matter how much telecommuting you do, there's always a requirement for face time, and they usually give you about twenty-four hours' notice," he says.

Still, the appeal here is increased, if not total, independence and control. Mr. Pohlman went solo six years ago, when the division of Chevron he worked for was sold and relocated. The myth of career security within the corporate womb was immediately apparent to him. He wasn't going to let some company control his destiny. "Downsizings always happen; interpersonal arguments in offices always turn into employment decisions later on," he says ruefully. "Stability wasn't a factor anymore."

Besides, as he thought about it, free agency seemed like a great career building opportunity. Flitting from project to project allowed him to diversify his work, gain broader knowledge of how companies operate, have a more extensive roster of business contacts, and get exposure to new technologies that would have been denied him in his narrow silo of a job at Chevron.

That's all terrific, if you're aiming for a corporate CEO job. Why else would you accumulate those kinds of experiences? To create a free agent company of your own, that's why. And Mr. Pohlman's company, Coradon Consulting of Tulsa, Oklahoma, is the very model of a modern free agent enterprise.

"People come to me and say, 'I like what you're doing and want to know how you're doing it,'" he says. "So I tell them, 'This is how I handle tax structure, benefits, legal responsibilities.' At that point, I give them a choice of staying with me or going out to form their own companies." Many stay for the cost-effectiveness and marketing synergy of collaborating. (I've seen this type of collaborative federation of free agents start to spread in recent years. Some examples: the Motley Fool, an icon of the free agent nation, which draws most of its analysis from its community of free agent analysts/"fools"; and about.com, which gathers together a community of experts on a variety of topics: Each is a free agent, in charge of his or her own site within the community.)

In building his company, Mr. Pohlman has used lessons he learned as a free agent on how companies operate—lessons, he says, he never would have been exposed to had he stayed in his narrow corporate job. He learned, for example, the importance of building bridges of respect among members of a company's various teams. "There's a lot of alienation among groups that don't understand each other," he says.

He doesn't rule out the possibility of one day using this cache of knowledge as a vice president or chief technology officer of some company that offers the right mix of staff chemistry, exciting new technology, and monetary gain. For now, though, his ever-expanding knowledge and contacts have positioned him as an ideal board member for technology start-ups. He currently sits on the boards of three companies and does so, he insists, "as a free agent."

He has also served as an interim executive on the payroll of client companies. In one, recently, he served for six months as an officer to help roll out a wireless portal server because the company's CTO didn't have enough time to devote to the project.

Mr. Pohlman relishes the independence of his role most of all. He recalls being brought in by the chief technology officer of a company to audit the proficiency of the corporate staff. The CTO felt he couldn't get a candid opinion internally.

This independence puts less strain on Mr. Pohlman's ethical values as well. He recalls working for an overseas-based company that wanted him to supply them with an encrypted financial system. Unfortunately, the company's country of origin wasn't on the State Department's approved list. "If I were an employee of the company, I would have been strongly encouraged to let it go," he says. "As a free agent, I could walk away."

But remember, this independence comes with a price tag. What doesn't? As a free agent, there are a number of chores that you now must take on, from the mundane (filing, secretarial work) to the critical (marketing, accounting, saving for retirement, insurance). "When you're an employee, a lot of that is handled for you, and that relieves a lot of stress," Mr. Pohlman says.

To help his company's associates deal with these issues, Mr. Pohlman gives all of them full access to his accountant and his customers. Could you imagine General Motors doing that for its employees? Now *that's* a free agent mentality.

To successfully become a free agent requires cultivating a free agent "mentality" before actually leaving the corporate womb.

49

GETTING BRANDED FOR LIFE

Personal branding has become a hot career topic of late. But like much of what's hot, I'm having a tough time taking this latest bit of "guruspeak" seriously. It seems to me that all that's happening is that people are putting a new label on an old concept.

For those who haven't heard about this particular concept, here it is in a nutshell: We should all build and promote our careers in the same way that Procter & Gamble builds a market for laundry detergent or Nike builds a market for athletic shoes. That is, by establishing in the mind of your consumer (in other words, employers) a brand image that will almost subliminally prompt them to hire you, promote you, and make you the godparent of their children. To "brand" your career, you must do two things: establish an image and then market that image.

The first task requires considerable time. Indeed, it is nothing less than the sum total of your performance throughout your career. And that includes the bad aspects as well as the good aspects. If you consistently perform a certain task, or set of tasks, you will develop an image as someone adept at those tasks. Have you become known as an innovator, a problem solver, a rainmaker, or a technology wizard? All of those are personal brands. You get them by delivering the goods consistently, so that eventually people recognize those qualities in you. This book is filled with people who have brand images—the turnaround artist, the corporate samurai, the hub, the technological go-to guy. But you had better be sure your own brand reflects good qualities. Continually underachieve, undermine colleagues, or suck up to the boss and you'll develop a brand image that neither you nor anyone else will like, but one that will be very difficult to shake. Remember "Chainsaw" Al Dunlop, the corporate executioner? He's got a brand name. But it isn't one you or I would ever want.

Now, it may have occurred to you in this brief description of what branding is all about that it sounds a lot like what most of us have known throughout our lives as "reputation." And you're right, that's exactly what it is. Of course, unless you give it a hip new name, you'll never get it on the covers of trendy business magazines and you won't be able to charge big fees to explain to people what it is. Still, if thinking about your reputation as a product brand helps you frame a conversation with yourself on your strengths and your career direction, who am I to quibble?

So what about the second part of your branding strategy, marketing the brand you've developed? The best brands are built over time, through word of mouth. People are impressed by a product, continue to use it repeatedly, and find that not only is it good, it's also reliable. The brand reaches its apotheosis when people begin recommending it to others. Of course, P&G and other big corporate marketers can give new brands a jump start in the marketplace by spending heavily to advertise and promote. But that isn't such a good idea for promoting a reputation. For one thing, you don't have the money to launch a major promotional campaign (if you did, you wouldn't need to do it). More important, though, the whole idea of career self-promotion gets pretty dicey. It's surprisingly easy to slide down that slippery slope into self-aggrandizement or filching credit for a subordinate's work. Many executives are thus loath to embrace the concept of branding, lest they be seen as tooting their own horns too loudly. I was told of a fast-track female executive at a major oil company who had developed her particular brand. But she wouldn't talk about it, fearful of a negative reaction from the company's other senior executives. There are, of course, ways to subtly market yourself to the people who matter. Take a look at the chapter titled "Getting Noticed Without Getting Pushy."

But what scares me most about the concept of branding—that is, actively marketing your reputation—is the possibility that it will stereotype you. That happened to Jim Blackwood. He had spent nearly fifteen years as a programmer for a health care data services company and recalls that he once said that "a successful career to me would be a large crowd of people saying, 'Jim Blackwood was the only guy who could help me out on this.'" If that isn't a brand, what is? He was the problem solver, the guy no manager can do without.

But that created a problem that Mr. Blackwood had some trouble solving: He was pigeonholed. He was such an indispensable problem solver, people couldn't envision him in another role. A year ago, when his boss was creating a new group, Mr. Blackwood interviewed for a manager's job. He was invited to be part of the group, but not as a manager. That's when he realized he needed to change his brand. "I was in a development rut," he says. "You have to occasionally reinvent yourself and evolve."

He finally broke through the brand barrier, mostly by accident. He was having lunch with an associate, a fellow who regularly scoured the company's open-position reports (his brand: reader of corporate tea leaves). His colleague mentioned a manager's job that was open, and Mr. Blackwood went after it. This time, interviewing with a stranger, he wasn't so encumbered by his brand and got his current job as manager of a network services engineering group. In truth, he says, the other job was probably a better fit in terms of skills and knowledge. Now he must fly blind a little more often and delegate more to his staff. In short, he has to build a new brand, this time as a motivating, positive manager. There are hurdles: he isn't very good at the minutiae of management, such as staff reports. But, he adds with some astonishment, "my current manager forgives me for a lot of my faults; he just tells me to keep focusing on the customer."

Branding your career is nothing more than establishing a reputation; let yours speak for itself.

50

LIFE AS A CORPORATE SAMURAI

He's known as a hired gun, mercenary, or corporate samurai. He swoops into a company to head a big project, fill in for a departed executive, or turn around an ailing operation. For those mired in the day-to-day grind of corporate life, the idea sounds downright swash-buckling. You dash in, save the day, rescue the fair maiden, and disappear in a cloud of dust and a hearty "Hi-yo, Silver!"

In recent years, the temporary executive or project manager has become a regular part of the corporate scene. He's still not the norm, but his (and her) numbers are growing. "For me, it's a great turn-on," says Werner von Pein, interim president of Lavazza Premium Coffee, the U.S. unit of the Italian coffee maker Lavazza SpA. At the time, he was wrapping up a decade as a temporary executive, and he says he planned to spend the rest of his career that way.

This career path can be rewarding financially as well as emotion-ally. Executive Interim Management, the agency that placed Mr. von Pein with Lavazza, says its temporary executives generally earn $1,000 to $1,500 a day.

Of course, being a corporate samurai isn't all thrills and big pay-days. These executives lead nomadic lives, getting shipped around the country on a regular basis. At the time, Mr. von Pein was working in

New York, not far from his Bridgeport, Connecticut, home. But he vividly recalls a previous assignment that required him to fly each Monday from Bridgeport to Philadelphia, change planes, jet to Atlanta, then drive for 3½ hours to the job site. He retraced his steps every Thursday.

Moreover, as with all temporary assignments, steady employment isn't assured. But then, permanent corporate employment isn't so certain anymore, either. Mr. von Pein endured numerous mergers and buyouts during his career as a full-time food industry executive with companies such as Quaker Oats, Procter & Gamble, and General Foods. He was a division executive during the zaniest buyout circus of them all—the much chronicled auction of RJR Nabisco. "Mentally, I've said, 'There's no guarantee anyway, so I might as well do something I enjoy,'" he says.

He joined Lavazza with a mandate to revive its U.S. operations after a profitless decade. Lavazza opted for a temporary chief in an attempt to "accelerate the turnaround," says Ernesto DiGiacomo, chief financial officer of the parent company and chairman of the U.S. unit. Part of Mr. von Pein's assignment is to define the traits needed in a permanent successor.

Those who flourish in this role enjoy living life on the run and in crisis mode. They learn quickly and are easily adaptable to different corporate cultures. They are "analytical, intuitive, and assertive," Mr. von Pein says. They are usually generalists, with a wide knowledge of various corporate functions. And they're willing to make decisions that won't necessarily win them friends.

The interim exec's first priority is to decide who are the keepers on staff and who must move on. Often, that's a major reason he's been brought on board, to relieve his permanent successor of the psychological baggage of such painful decisions. Theoretically, that's an easier task for a temporary executive, who doesn't have the emotional ties to the staff of a full-timer. Mr. von Pein evaluated his people during meetings, where he felt he could quickly determine who were clear thinkers, what they considered important, and how they approached problems. It also showed him how well they handled themselves in front of a group and under pressure.

Operational and personnel decisions must be made quickly. The pressure on the corporate samurai is to complete the assignment—whether it's a turnaround or the launching of a new product—and return the company to normal footing as quickly as possible.

Without the luxury of time, the temporary executive must identify problems early on, meaning he or she will undoubtedly endure long hours and ceaseless conversations across all parts of the operation. Mr. von Pein, for example, quickly unearthed the fact that salespeople were making commitments to customers on payment terms, rebates, and other financial issues without informing the financial department. "The salespeople had no idea of the implications for the bottom line" of these commitments, he says.

Now the sales and financial managers meet regularly.

For those interested in this kind of career path, there are a growing number of agencies handling temporary assignments for managers. If you prefer periodic adrenaline surges to "steady as she goes" career development, you might want to look into them.

If you're willing—and able—to take on the tough cases, more and more companies are looking for executive commandos to swoop in and rescue ailing operations.

51

BUILDING A PARALLEL CAREER
FOR FUN AND PROFIT

You've got a career itch. Maybe you're questioning the direction your career is headed. Or there's just something out there you've always wanted to do.

But you're not one of those go-for-broke entrepreneurs, and the itch you want to scratch isn't a billion-dollar idea. What do you do?

For an increasing number of people these days, the answer lies in pursuing a parallel career. Take C. B. Bowman, for instance. When I first talked to her, she had a full-time job as manager in the visual communications department of a big consumer products company.

But when her workday ends, she really gets busy, running her own career management firm, working as a counselor for an outplacement firm, and lecturing at nearby Mercy College on organizational behavior and human resources management. Oh yes, she was working on two books, too.

Her multiple career paths provided Ms. Bowman with security. If her day job went away, she would just put more of her time into her other endeavors and keep on trucking. No lengthy job search; no financial anxiety over a layoff.

Besides, she sees this as a preferred way of life. "I have always believed one should have more than one career," she says. Ten years earlier, when she had but one job, she was miserable, with "not enough to do to hold my interest."

Now, people have frequently held down two or more jobs in order to make ends meet, but this is something far more ambitious: working simultaneous jobs, any of which could at any time be developed into a full-time career. Their ranks are growing as more people seek independent, free agent careers and find that it takes several career pieces to make it work.

Many find this a compelling long-term lifestyle, a way to combat creeping corporate ennui or to fill voids in their professional lives. That's the way it was for Scott Adams, a Pacific Telesis technician who wanted to scratch a creative itch. By the time his longtime employer decided his services were no longer needed, Mr. Adams's popular syndicated comic strip, *Dilbert,* had become a runaway hit, making him a wealthy man.

Doug Crawford put together a parallel career by linking different jobs related to his philosophy on spirituality in the workplace. He established ties with consulting groups dealing with various aspects of the spiritual needs of the individual and the organization. Meanwhile, he is doing some public speaking and writing.

"I'm putting enough pieces together so I'll never have to return to the corporate world," he says.

But parallel careers aren't easy. And they aren't for everybody. Mr. Crawford first attempted a parallel career structure in 1990, abandoning his job as a finance executive for PepsiCo's Frito-Lay unit because he wanted his work to reflect the spiritual transformation he was undergoing. But financial setbacks forced him to return to the corporate world full-time in 1995. A year later, he set off again.

To succeed at it requires abundant energy, extraordinary time management skills, and lots of the so-called self skills—self-discipline, self-sacrifice, self-marketing, and enough self-awareness to know your limits. The longer hours and heavier workloads people bear at work these days doesn't make it any easier.

Clearly, you can't think of it as just another job or a way to pick up extra money. This isn't like picking up some loose change by working the Christmas rush at Macy's. It has to be something you're driven to do, or you simply won't devote the time and energy needed to make it work.

Ms. Bowman's parallel jobs all could become career replacements someday and thus require a "real serious commitment," she says. She works most evenings and weekends and uses her vacation time for work or study related to her other careers.

You also must be wary of engaging in anything that would conflict with your full-time job. Ask yourself, Will my boss have a problem with this? "You don't want your nine-to-five employer to feel you're taking unfair advantage of the knowledge you've developed there," Ms. Bowman says.

There's also a real danger of burnout. Some people try to start two new things at once—a bad idea—or maintain a heart-attack-inducing pace to build up business in their alternate career too quickly. So avoid taking on too much, and develop some emotional releases. For Mr. Crawford, it's time spent with his son. For Ms. Bowman, it's her country home, paid for with her extra income. "I do some gardening, listen to the birds," she says. "It's extremely rewarding and relaxing."

Until you "get in a groove," Ms. Bowman adds, managing multiple careers can be highly stressful; those undergoing some other crisis in their lives, or who are already feeling overwhelmed at work, don't need the extra headaches.

To create time for her added endeavors, Ms. Bowman vowed to boost her productivity and eliminate time wasted at the office. She started taking more work home, for example. "I can knock out a report in one-quarter of the time it takes in the office," she claims. "I'm not answering the phone, and people aren't coming in and asking questions."

Now there's an interesting thought. What if the pursuit of parallel careers made you a better manager, more willing to delegate, more efficient with your time? Even if your parallel careers flopped, that residual benefit would make it worthwhile.

It isn't for everyone, but running a parallel career allows some people to indulge a dream while providing themselves with a fallback career.

52

IT'S NOT WHERE YOU START,
IT'S WHERE YOU END UP

As you've seen throughout this book, the road to career success in corporate America isn't necessarily a straight and predictable one, and there are no cookie-cutter maps for that road. There are, in fact, many roads from which to choose. And even if your ambition is the oldest one in the book—rising to the top of some corporate monolith— there's no single way to get there. Sure, there are plenty of Harvard MBA hares out there, racing toward the corner office, but there are quite a few tortoises out there, too, who have come from unexpected places to reign over giant organizations.

Darryl Hartley-Leonard came to the United States from England in 1964, fresh from hotel school and confident a U.S. hotel company would snap him up as a general manager. Several rejections later, he was hired as a desk clerk at a Los Angeles Hyatt Hotel.

His relationship with Pat Foley, the general manager, changed his life. The shy Englishman copied his gregarious boss's style and mannerisms. He learned how to treat employees from Mr. Foley, who washed dishes with the kitchen help and cosigned an $800 note for Mr. Hartley-Leonard's first car. And as Mr. Foley's career prospered, so did Mr. Hartley-Leonard's. When Mr. Foley became the resident manager at Hyatt's first big hotel in Atlanta, he hired Mr. Hartley-

Leonard as a front-office supervisor. Mr. Foley eventually became president and installed his protégé as executive vice president. Mr. Hartley-Leonard eventually became chief executive officer.

Not surprisingly, Mr. Hartley-Leonard considers mentoring a critical element in his ascent. "If you get five people of equal ability, the one who gets mentoring will have the edge," he says. And Hyatt's corporate culture is built on a "develop and promote your own" philosophy. Some Hyatt managers don't have college degrees, Mr. Hartley-Leonard says.

Ivan Seidenberg, the son of an air-conditioning and refrigeration contractor in the Bronx, joined the New York Telephone Co., which became Nynex, in 1966 because other employers wouldn't hire someone with a 1A draft status. "I didn't have a career path in mind," he says. "I wanted to finish school." After a two-year army stint, he returned to the company and earned a steady stream of promotions. What was his big break? "Most people would say it was in 1982, when I was named a team leader of one of five task forces assigned to break up the Bell system," he says. "I had to make presentations, got tested by people, had to compromise, debate issues. I got exposure to all the senior people."

But personally, he points to his "somewhat unheard-of" job switch from the regional phone company to AT&T in 1971. "That move forced me to grow faster than I would have," he explains. "The general level of the workforce was different, and I was thrust into very broad issues."

The regulatory, competitive, and legal issues he learned led to his role in the AT&T breakup. It also led to the elimination of his job. But by then he'd developed a lot of contacts and knowledge about the coming era of deregulation. "There was no question that what I'd done was going to be valuable to someone, AT&T or the competition," he says.

He returned to Nynex in 1984 as assistant VP for regulatory affairs, and seven promotions later, he became CEO. He credits, among other things, bosses who believed in his ability to handle tough assignments even when he wasn't sure, and a knack for translating technical jargon into plain English for colleagues. Mostly, though, he credits landing the right assignments.

To get them, he says, you need a powerful supporter. And how do you get one? Mr. Seidenberg cites the advice of two early bosses: Work hard to be the most knowledgeable person at any job you do, and be a positive person whom senior managers are comfortable being around.

Those bits of advice "don't guarantee success," he says, "but not knowing your stuff and being a pain in the neck is an absolute prescription for failure."

My favorite mailroom-to-boardroom success story is that of Bill Woodard, who while in high school pictured a future as a mechanic or postman. "I really thought my career would be blue-collar," he says. "I just didn't see the value of college in my life at the time."

Now, at age forty-nine, it's Dr. Woodard, if you please, president of ACS Government Solutions Group, a Rockville, Maryland, technology services company with $650 million in annual sales. How did he do it? With insightful mentors, a renewed hunger for learning, and a persistent desire to better himself.

In 1969, he got a tip that the Census Bureau was hiring computer operators, a job that required a high school degree. He took the GED, got his diploma, and started his career at the bottom rung of civil service—a step below mail messengers.

Once on the job, he found another good reason to return to school: Students could avoid rotating shifts. He started at community college, then transferred to a full-time program at the University of Maryland in 1973. Meanwhile, he found work on the night shift at the Export-Import Bank, a job that required some light programming. "I found that I truly loved doing that," he says. "I enjoyed the art, working the algorithms, writing the payroll programs."

At the Ex-Im, he met Joe Magyar, a concentration camp survivor, self-made senior executive, and powerful role model. Mr. Magyar persuaded him to switch to days so the young man could hone his management skills, working with customers and with the organization's benefits and human resources staffs.

"He had a wonderful saying," his protégé recalls. "'A cooked goose doesn't just fly into your mouth.'"

In 1982, while running a tech center for Computer Sciences Corp., he read in notices for new projects that a master's degree was worth three added years of experience for those seeking a coveted program manager's job. "That didn't mean you had to have one, but it showed they valued it," he says. "That pushed me over the edge."

He earned his master's in engineering technology management in 1988 from Johns Hopkins and immediately was given a big assignment to salvage an underperforming operation. "It did me a lot of good within the company to be able to turn around a troubled situation," he says.

By 1990, he was a vice president and working toward a doctorate in education and management, which he earned in 1991. By now a believer in lifelong learning, he took an advanced management program at Duke and was loaned out for one year as an executive for Britain's Inland Revenue.

He came away with a greater appreciation for U.S. management style and the belief that the difference between effective and ineffective managers was just two or three decisions a year. "You don't make a decision every day that impacts the organization, so you have to recognize the ones that do and focus on them," he says. "In a bureaucracy, there's a tendency to treat every problem the same."

He was recruited by Affiliated Computer Services in 1997 while convalescing from a motorcycle crash. He was intrigued by the opportunity to work for and eventually succeed Pete Bracken, president of the Government Solutions Group and a respected industry executive. He also was intrigued by the parent company's CEO, Jeff Rich, a thirty-nine-year-old contrarian who was buying defense-related businesses when everyone else was jumping overboard. Here, he figured, was another opportunity to learn.

"It was always important to me whom I worked with," says Dr. Woodard, who became president of the unit in July 1999. It's not just looking for buddies, he adds. You want a degree of partnership, and "you want to see the tenets of good business in your leadership: trust, openness, integrity—all those words people put on their cards."

Dr. Woodard also has a message for late bloomers like himself. His doctoral dissertation at Virginia Tech focused on people who succeeded in their careers past forty years of age. The keys: They were insatiably curious, accepted the need for change, often faced a situation where luck or crisis (a layoff or relocation, perhaps) spurred them to pursue new things, and had a sage manager or mentor. "Almost all of those had played a part in my career," he says.

The four factors that can propel you to the top of the corporate ladder: ability, attention-getting assignments, powerful sponsors, and, most important of all as you near the tip of the pyramid, plain, old-fashioned luck.

ACKNOWLEDGMENTS

This book would not have been possible without all the people who have advised, supported, and nagged me until it was done. First, my thanks to Fred Hills of Simon & Schuster and Doug Sease of *The Wall Street Journal,* my editors. Their unflagging support, patience, and sage counsel kept me going in the right direction. My family was also an inspiration. My wife, Sue, and sons, Merrit and Mitchell, provided me with all the motivation I needed and my mom, Ann Lancaster, gave me my inquisitive nature and sense of humor.

I'd also like to thank the two great teachers and mentors in my life: my high school journalism teacher, Ralph Rothrock, that rare teacher who encourages and inspires and whose influence extends far beyond the high school years, and my first *Wall Street Journal* boss, Bill Blundell, the kind of patient and wise first boss everybody needs and the best teacher of writing I've ever known. Thanks also to Rachellee Chandler, who sacrificed a summer vacation from the University of Texas to help a harried and disorganized neighbor make sense out of five years of notes, files, and research. And to Greg Hill, my colleague and longtime friend, who had nothing to do with this book, but a great deal to do with my career over the years. He always complained that I never thanked him. Consider yourself thanked.

Finally, my heartfelt thanks to all the people whose career stories are chronicled herein; if this book provides any benefit, it is largely because of their time, trust, and candor.

INDEX

ABOUT THE AUTHOR

HAL LANCASTER has spent thirty years at *The Wall Street Journal* as a reporter, editor, bureau chief, and columnist. From 1994 through 1999, he wrote the *Journal*'s weekly "Managing Your Career" column and now writes "Career Corner," a twice-monthly feature for the acclaimed CareerJournal.com website. He lives in Los Alamitos, California, with his wife and two sons.